D1266116

SUITE TALK:

A Guide to Business Excellence

Dan Burdakin

To: A friend of Khuan's Hair Designs,
Hope you enjoy the book - Best Wishes!

Dan Burdakin

Foreword by Art Fettig

Library of Congress Control Number: 2003091931

Burdakin, Dan
Suite talk: a guide to business excellence / by Dan Burdakin.
P.cm.
ISBN 0-9740094-0-7

FIRST EDITION

10 9 8 7 6 5 4 3 2 1

Suite Talk

Lead Goose Publishing Company
P. O. Box 70666
Marietta, GA 30007-0666

To Mom and Dad.

To my loving wife Cheryl.

To my daughter Nicole.

To my brothers, John and David.

To all of my extended family and friends.

Special Thanks to These Organizations...

I would like to offer my special thanks and appreciation to the following enterprises that have contributed to my personal experience and knowledge base from which this book was envisioned and created:

AirTran Airways
Art Cleaners
Buddy's Pizza
Continental Airlines
Drury Hotels
Electronic Data Systems
Grand Trunk Western Railroad Company
Heartland Express
Hightower Trail Middle School
Homestead Studio Suites Hotels
HON Company
Khuan's Hair Designs
La Quinta Inns & Suites
McDonald's Restaurants
Michigan State University
Nordstrom
Pike Place Fish
Red Roof Inns
Ritz-Carlton Hotel Company
Singapore Airlines
Southwest Airlines
Taco Bell Restaurants
Waffle House Restaurants
Wainwright Industries
Wal-Mart
Walt Disney Company
World Cinema

CONTENTS

Foreword

A long time ago Dan Burdakin's father, John Burdakin, who was then President of the railroad I worked for, taught me a great way to make introductions. You find out as much as you can about both of the parties you are introducing and then you sell them on one another; on their accomplishments, their talents, on what makes them special. It makes both parties feel great and it really helps people get to know one another quickly.

It is a wonderful technique because it demands that you look for the good in everyone you meet.

I'm sort of at a disadvantage, not knowing you, the reader, personally. I can make a few assumptions though, since you now have this book in your hands. I'd guess that you are either in some way connected with the hotel business and you want to climb to the head of your field, or, you are one of those successful people who realize that most of the really great, break-through ideas come from outside your own field.

Probably you have observed that in almost any field here in America, and throughout the world today, the bar has been raised and if we hope to succeed and thrive then we must discover and maintain a whole new level of excellence.

If I have you pegged right then you are going to love Dan Burdakin and his book, _Suite Talk_.

I first met Dan when he was still in high school and his dad sent him over to meet me. We shared an interest in photography and we spent a day together wandering around the railroad. He wanted to know about everything and we shot up a couple of rolls of film together. He had a good eye for pictures and for people.

Then Dan went on to become a tremendous success in the hotel industry. He took my book, _Selling Lucky_, along with him and it started him out in a quest for great ideas that work.

He has been sharing great ideas with his business associates and with customers all his life and his book, _Suite Talk_, is crammed full of field tested concepts that made him so successful in the hotel industry.

It is an easy read. In fact, it is hard to put down, but the chapters are short so that you can just pick it up when you have a few moments and go away with an idea that will spin around in your head and demand action.

I predict that you will read this book from cover to cover and then you will go out and buy another copy for a friend. You will want to keep your own copy because it is the kind of book that you will return to over the years and when you do return to it will seem like a brand new book. Of course, the book won't change but both times and you will change and then you will find many applications for the ideas it presents. The concepts are so strong that they will endure.

So now that the two of you have met, I hope you will truly enjoy each other's company. I honestly believe that this book will help you move up a notch or two yourself and make it possible for you to not only cope with the changes and challenges we meet but to enjoy the journey as well.

-Art Fettig, Author of _"Selling Lucky"_, _"Winning the Safety Commitment"_ and _"It Only Hurts When I Frown"_

Introduction

"Try not. Do or do not. There is no try."
-Yoda, Jedi Knight Trainer Teaching Luke Skywalker in *"The Empire Strikes Back"*

Have you noticed that the speed and intensity of business has recently accelerated to near *Star Wars* proportion? Everyone wants things accomplished faster, cheaper and better. We want information and results...now! No more *trying*, we need to *do* it and *make things happen!*

As the years have passed by, I have found myself running increasingly short on time teaching and communicating the many valuable lessons that I have learned in the past twenty-plus years as an executive manager in the hotel industry. *Suite Talk - A Guide to Business Excellence* was written to communicate and teach these leadership secrets in a faster, cheaper and better manner that is sure to provide immediate positive results for any reader.

Chris Silver, a hotel manager in the Raleigh, North Carolina area once described to me how a plate juggler that he had seen at a circus reminded him of the key to business success. He described this plate juggler as one who had ten or more plates and he would set them on sharp sticks and begin to spin them. By the time he got to plate five he would have to go back to the first plate that was beginning to wobble. The juggler began running back and forth to keep plates from falling on the floor. However, he didn't do so well. When he got to the tenth plate; 1, 2, 3, 4, and 5 began to fall on the floor. The plate juggler failed, but taught this important lesson...we can't do everything, but we can do a few things well.

The same principle that applies to the plate juggler applies to all businesses and organizations. By keeping things simple and concentrating on successfully balancing just a handful of *key result areas*, we can achieve *business excellence*.

This book is broken down into four *key result areas - Quality, Service, Teamwork & Profitability*. One might think of each of these being a leg of a four-legged chair with the seat of the chair being integrity. With all of these items in balance, success is certain to be achieved. Also, because of the importance of always giving something *extra*, you will find an additional section entitled, *And Then Some...*, too!

Before we get going, I want you to know that I believe in *win-win* partnerships. I have spent a lot of time pulling these "thoughts" together to share with you in this book. You, on the other hand, are going to invest your time in reading this material and I want the experience to be a "10" for you.

What does being a "10" mean? Well, in the hotel business we frequently put a guest comment card on the bed and it lets the guest rate the facility, product and service from "1 to 10". Naturally, we want to be the very best we can be for all of our guests and so we want to be a "10". Anytime we fall short of our goal of being a "10", we want to know about it so we can immediately take actions to improve whatever obstacle is in the way of achieving the success we desire.

The same is true of our team members...we want their employment experience to be a "10", as well. When completing a new hire's orientation, it is important to communicate this philosophy of being a "10" to them because they share in the responsibility of letting us know if we ever fall short of being a "10". Rather than be unhappy and unproductive, they need to let us know so we can *fix it*.

Okay, applying this to *Suite Talk*, the deal is that I want this book to be a "10" for you and will do whatever it takes to make it a valuable, usable tool for managing both your business and your career. If at any time you don't understand something, have a question, or if you would just like some further explanation of any key principle contained herein, please send me an e-mail to burdakinhotels@aol.com, and I will make it right for you. Your satisfaction is *guaranteed*.

Finally, getting back to our *win-win* partnership...I am interested in sharing your experiences with others. You see, the lessons in *Suite Talk* pertain to areas far broader than just the hospitality industry. For instance, learning to smile and be friendly applies to doctors, teachers and everyone in a people related business. Imagine what a happier, nicer and better service-oriented world it can be! Please send me any stories that you have which pertain to the fundamentals expressed in this book. Again, these should be sent via e-mail to burdakinhotels@aol.com, and I promise to acknowledge all correspondence received.

Now, get ready for some *Suite Talk*...

I. Quality

"We are what we repeatedly do. Excellence is therefore not an act, but a habit."
-Aristotle, Greek Philosopher, 384-322 B.C.

"I want our teams to get better every day. If we can do that, the other stuff will take care of itself. And also, I have a private goal of being consistently excellent."
-Mike Kryzewski, Coach of Duke University's Men's Basketball Team

"Even if you are on the right track, you'll get run over if you just sit there."
-Will Rogers, 1879-1935, American Humorist, Actor

"I don't want someone on the East Coast getting on an airplane to the West Coast and eating Domino's pizza again and having a totally different experience."
-Dave Brandon, Chairman & CEO of Domino's Pizza

"I only hope that we don't lose sight of one thing - that it was all started by a mouse."
-Walt Disney, 1901-1966, Co-Founder of The Disney Company

Chapter 1 - Mint on the Pillow; Hole in the Sheet

"Stress your strengths, emphasize quality service, cleanliness, and value, and the competition will wear itself out trying to keep up."
-Ray Kroc, the late founder of McDonald's Restaurants

In 1977, I entered my freshman year at Michigan State University's *The* School of Hospitality Business. There were many AWESOME professors (Ronald F. Cichy, Michael Kasavana, Raymond Schmidgall, to name a few), yet my first experience with Don Smith is what I remember most.

You see, Don Smith was the new head of MSU's School of Hotel, Restaurant and Institutional Management (one of the nation's top educational programs) and he was scheduled to meet and address our class of eager, ready to conquer-the-world students. So little did we really know!

Don suddenly charged into the room, tossed his coat aside, rolled up his sleeves and announced his concern regarding our potential ability to be successful in the hospitality business. This skepticism was the result of his having walked the hallways of Eppley Business Center for two days and nobody had even offered a brief *"Hi"* to him. Don told us that the most basic rule in any business that deals with people was to say *"Hi"* and smile at total strangers. We sat there in shock, like deer frozen in oncoming headlights with eyes wide-open.

At that point we realized that the *basics* come *first*. Forget about books and lectures until the simple act of greeting everyone within sight with a *"Hi"* and a smile was mastered. As H. Jackson Brown, Jr. said, *"Remember, it is not your job to get people to like you; it's your job to like people."*

In my many years since Don Smith taught our class about basics, I have been amazed at how important this lesson is to the success of any business that deals with people. Constantly, people are sidetracked by ambitious, fancy ideas and lose sight of the basics. Quality is doing *first things first*.

To give you an example of this as it pertains to the hotel industry, I have frequently been told by well-intentioned middle management that we could improve both our quality and service by adding amenities such as placing a mint on a pillow in each guest room prior to arrival. Whenever I hear such a recommendation, my face tends to automatically scrunch up and I remember back to a story told to me by a friend of our family, motivational speaker Art Fettig.

Art Fettig, author of both *It Only Hurts When I Frown* and *Selling Lucky*, once told me of an experience that he had while staying at a downtown hotel in Flint, Michigan. Though a popular, brand-name facility it had holes in the walls. The sheets had burn holes, the bedspread had a big tear and the rug was a mess. Pitiful. Art went to try out the hot tub facility and there were about a thousand bugs flying in the air above it. Really.

The next day when he arrived back home, Art had a letter and an advertisement from the hotel chain's president telling him of their fantastic hotels. He wrote him and told him that while there might have been a mint on the pillow, the rest of his experience was dreadful. Eventually, Art received word that he would be hearing from the hotel manager. After a couple of months Art wrote back and said he had not been called. Finally, a fellow called, introduced himself as the manager, and acknowledged that everything that Art had experienced was true and that because the hotel was losing so much money, they couldn't provide even the basics.

The point is that no matter what, the basics come first. In the hotel industry, this means a clean, safe product delivered by caring team members. In other professions, consistently delivering the basics executed flawlessly is similarly the key to success in terms of quality management. Take for instance, the businesses of hair design and dry cleaning.

A little over five years ago, our family moved from Fort Worth, Texas to Atlanta, Georgia. Moving is a big-time deal and always involves a lot of change. Two important decisions would be finding a new place to get a hair cut, and where to get our clothes dry-cleaned. After a couple of flawed experiments with various local shops, I was lucky to meet Khuan of *Khuan's Hair Design,* as well as the family at *Art Cleaners.* Both of these small businesses operate with 100% quality and always get the basics right. In all the time that I have known them, appointments have been kept, services delivered and we have never had a garment returned with a broken button or problem. Double WOW...these folks exemplify excellence every day. That is why we now go *"out of the way"* to continue to do business with them, despite having since moved to another house several miles further away.

Jeff Shannon, a sports fan and very personable hotel manager in the St. Louis area, once sent me a newspaper clipping that further highlights this principle. It was a couple of years ago, and Tony LaRussa, baseball manager of the St. Louis Cardinals, explained slugger Mark McGwire's swing and record setting season of 70 home runs, *"The power comes from the feet up."* To start at the *feet* in the business arena means to master the *basics* and put *first things first.*

WE CAN MAKE A · WORLD OF DIFFERENCE

Chapter 2 - Becoming "World Class"

"Character is doing what's right when nobody is watching."
-Colin Powell, U. S. Secretary of State

Over the past two decades, more and more businesses have found themselves competing in a global economy. For long-term success, it is no longer good enough to be the best on the block, the best in the city, or the best in the state. These days, one must continually improve on an ongoing basis and make certain that no one, anywhere in the world, does what you do better than you do it. You must be *"world class."*

Becoming *"world class"* is difficult, but there are some very simple and easy-to-use tools that can help any organization along the quality journey to success. The first is the Malcolm Baldrige National Quality Award program, established by Congress in 1987, and managed by the National Institute of Standards and Technology (NIST), an agency of the U.S. Department of Commerce.

Named after the 26th Secretary of Commerce, the Malcolm Baldrige National Quality Award was developed to enhance the international competitiveness of businesses and organizations located within the United States. It concentrates on seven areas: leadership, strategic planning, customer and market focus, information and analysis, human resource focus, process management, and business results.

When I first became aware of the Baldrige Award process, it was when *The Ritz-Carlton Hotel Company* was the initial service organization to win this prestigious honor back in 1992. Being in the hospitality industry, I naturally began to study what Ritz-Carlton had done to become the very *best*.

The first thing that I learned about Ritz-Carlton and the Malcolm Baldrige National Quality Award was that it isn't important that you actually win the award. Yes, for the very first time in my life I realized that just competing in a *"world class"* arena was more important than holding up a trophy. While I am sure that those who work at Ritz-Carlton were happy to receive this honor, and later a second award in 1999, with the Baldrige Award the victory is actually in the self-assessment and improvement process. Whether or not anyone is actually watching, just being the best one can be, continuous improvement and doing the right thing is success.

In regards to self-assessment, the Baldrige National Quality Program offers several free guides and questionnaires to help one assess their own business and to develop action plans leading to performance excellence. These can easily be obtained on the NIST website, www.quality.nist.gov and are designed to enhance the competitiveness, quality, and productivity of U.S. organizations for the benefits of all residents.

The next most important tool to utilize along the quality journey is to benchmark with acknowledged leaders within both the same and other industries. For instance, though I am a hotelier and visited Ritz-Carlton, I also visited Wainwright Industries in St. Peters, Missouri shortly after they received the Missouri Quality Award and immediately before they won the 1994 Malcolm Baldrige National Quality Award.

Wainwright Industries is a family owned business that manufactures stamped and machine parts in the automotive, aerospace, home-security and information-processing industries. I was drawn to them due to their excellence in the area of continuous improvement by constantly searching for, and implementing, ideas on how to streamline processes.

During my visit to Wainwright Industries, I learned how systems could be developed to draw input from all levels of the organization and lead to heightened customer satisfaction ratings. Suggestions for improvement were elicited from all their associates and everyone was fully engaged in quality efforts. That year, the average Wainwright team member actually *implemented* 54 ideas for improvement.

Prior to evaluating Wainwright, I had found myself encouraging subordinates to concentrate suggestions in areas that were frequently outside of their control. This was not nearly as effective as their program of focusing on those items that were within the team member's immediate work space and having all suggestions formally responded to within 24 hours of submission. Wainwright's associates also benefited from their own good ideas - in the form of increased profit-sharing and improved workplace safety.

Even though Wainwright Industries is in the manufacturing business, benchmarking with them created many positive changes within the hotels that I supervised. Things such as improving locations of supplies (linen, towels, soap, vacuum cleaners, etc.) led to reduced cycle time and increased profits. Better yet, when a *"world class"* work environment exists, turnover rates are lowered and team members have much higher levels of enjoyment and job satisfaction.

Another neat thing about world class organizations, such as Ritz-Carlton and Wainwright Industries, is that they want to help everyone improve. They share information because they know it will raise-the-bar even higher and continue to challenge themselves and heighten levels of performance. Don't be afraid to ask any winner of a Baldrige Quality Award for assistance because they will be more than happy to help you, and your business, achieve greater results.

Chapter 3 - The Cost of Quality

"Is Buddy's the best pizza? It sure is, because it is the one that all the others are compared to."
-Bob Talbert, former Detroit Free Press columnist

Once a business has determined that the basics are successfully maintained, through both self-assessment and benchmarking processes, the next big challenge is making sure that quality goals have the same importance as marketing and financial goals.

Organizations who subscribe to the belief that high quality values are essential and also that the achievement of quality objectives will in-turn drive the financial goals are those who will be most successful in current times. The "cost of quality" can easily be seen through analyzing the value of a customer, what percentage of customers are not satisfied, and the percentage of customers who will not return due to errors made.

It seems pretty simple, yet many times throughout my career in the hotel business it seemed that the leaders focused on occupancy and rate figures alone. Quality frequently took a backseat to the latest marketing plan and/or the latest financial results. While I was originally frustrated by this, Steve Bollinger, a mentor and friend, taught me that it was my responsibility to convince the top-level executives of the reason to implement initiatives that I would propose. The only obstacle was myself and my ability, or inability, to do so. It wasn't their fault. The responsibility was mine. This paradigm change was key to future success. Looking inward and quantifying future initiatives in terms of the "cost of quality" helped me, and will help you, sleep better at night.

Let me give an example of the importance of quality in driving financial results. It is one that I think that everyone can understand because it involves something as simple as pizza. No really, pizza! The best pizza in the entire world. The pizza of *Buddy's Restaurant/Pizzeria* at Six Mile and Conant Roads in Detroit, Michigan.

In 1977, my best friends, Jeff & Mary Kay Laskowsky, told me about Buddy's and on a snowy night in Motown we ventured out to experience why this relatively small business, established in 1936, was consistently voted the #1 square deep dish pizza in Detroit. The answer was absolutely delicious and based on Buddy's total commitment to quality.

Buddy's is the best. The reasons why are relatively simple and explained on their website, www.buddyspizza.com. First, Buddy's makes their dough from scratch daily, using only premium grade flour, carefully double kneading the dough and allowing it to rise for over an hour to help create the famous crunchy crust. Next, they use almost one pound of cheese on Buddy's 8-square pizzas and this brick cheese is made especially for Buddy's in Wisconsin and is shredded by hand for the perfect melt.

Getting hungry, yet? Well, there is even more to Buddy's commitment to quality. Buddy's receives their produce daily and hand-slices all of their vegetable toppings. The pizza sauce is made with a blend of Stanislaus premium tomato products, herbs and spices and they use Margherita brand pepperoni - a lean, high quality, more flavorful course ground sausage placed meticulously under the cheese to prevent charring from the high baking heat. And one final thing, ALL of Buddy's black steel pizza pans are specially seasoned and some have been around for more than 50 years.

Now, Buddy's could surely use cheaper ingredients and cut costs by not spending so much on their labor-intensive process. But this is where the "cost of quality" comes in. If they were to do so, they would become just another pizza place that can be found on any street corner in America. Not Buddy's, they have a commitment to quality and are the best and it is no surprise to me that Buddy's has now expanded to nine locations throughout Metropolitan Detroit.

The other day, I was home in Atlanta discussing Buddy's with my wife and commiserating with her regarding our inability to find anything even close to their pizza in Georgia. Worse, my job responsibilities have recently changed and I no longer visit Detroit (and Buddy's) on such a frequent basis. Since 1977, I estimate that I have spent $6,000 at Buddy's (spending an average of $20 per month over 25 years). That is what the "cost of quality" is all about. If Buddy's was a run-of-the-mill pizza establishment I wouldn't have spent nearly this amount and they probably wouldn't have realized the potential they had to create a devoted, lifetime customer.

So, I decided to e-mail Buddy's and told them how much I missed their pizza and asked for an alternative suggestion in the Atlanta area. The next morning I received a phone call at home. It was Dennis Kot, manager of the original Buddy's on Six Mile and Conant Roads. He told me that he would be happy to half-bake and freeze some and ship them to me. He told me that it isn't uncommon for ex-Detroiters to miss Buddy's so much that they ask him to do this, even ordering as many as eleven pizzas! Well, I ordered several large pizzas and they arrived perfectly intact, along with directions for preparation attached. We were delighted to have the world's best pizza for dinner, and I bet Buddy's was also delighted that I had now spent another $100 at their place of business, strictly because of their commitment to quality!

Chapter 4 - Establish Win-Win Partnerships

"I find the great thing in this world is not so much where we stand, as in what direction we are moving."
-Oliver Wendell Holmes, 1809-1894, U.S. Physician, Poet, Humorist

It has been said that the key to success and total quality management is, *"Not doing one thing 100 percent better, but rather doing 100 things one percent better"*. In today's difficult economy and fierce competitive environment, organizations must constantly strive for continuous improvement in all areas. It is true now more than ever that if a business isn't getting better, it is getting worse.

One key area of opportunity for improvement that exists within most companies is the development of partnerships with not only internal and external customers, but also with suppliers. To be effective going forward, we must realize the important role that every component of a business offers and embrace the philosophy that no ingredient of a cake is the most important…miss one and the whole cake is ruined. Supplier relationships are a critical ingredient to success.

When I was just starting out in the hotel business, I initially believed that dealings with suppliers were adversarial situations. After all, they were always trying to sell me things and make as much profit as possible while I was interested in getting high quality at the absolute lowest cost possible. They wanted me to spend more, and I wanted to spend less. It certainly would seem that these two opposite objectives were destined from the start to clash and be at odds with one another. While I always treated guests, clients and co-worker's of the hotels as if they were part of the family, dealing with suppliers was a whole different ballgame.

Over time, I learned that it didn't have to be that way. Some of my suppliers actually were interested in helping me achieve my business objectives. By sharing information and resources, we began to develop win-win partnerships. By understanding each other's objectives, we became committed to working through all issues and also develop future opportunities together. Letting suppliers know that they were part of our family, and just as important to us as our guests, clients and co-workers were, we established partnerships that would improve efficiencies, quality and, in many cases, actually reduce expenses.

Now, don't get me wrong. There are some suppliers out there that may not share your belief and commitment to total quality management and/or developing long-lasting relationships. You need to take inventory of your suppliers and determine who you want to become partners with, and who doesn't fit your vision. While the hope is that everyone can become a partner, sometimes that isn't the case. Let me give you an example of a situation where I had to regretfully send one supplier packing.

Years ago, I was visiting a hotel within my region and reviewing the expense portion of their profit and loss statement. Sticking out like a sore thumb was the fact that the trash removal expense had continually increased over the past 12 months. It started out at $180/month and was now costing $360/month. At the same time, a competitor of our waste removal vendor had coincidentally just dropped-off a proposal to give us the same service for $163/month.

Now, I don't like to change suppliers. It goes against everything that I believe in about creating partnerships. So, I called up our existing trash removal vendor who quickly agreed to come out and meet with me. The salesperson who arrived went on and on about increased landfill costs. He also said that all price increases were mentioned in fine print on the invoice the month prior to occurring. If we had called and objected, they wouldn't have raised the price.

So, I told him that I had another vendor that would provide the same service at half the expense and I didn't like a company trying to sneak price increases in whenever we didn't pick up the phone and object. Our relationship was coming to an end. Immediately he objected and said he had a signed contract committing us to his company for five (5) years. I demanded to see it and he pulled it out and handed it to me. The contract wasn't signed and I handed it back to him and told him to leave. He then quickly offered to match the $163 price, but it was too late...I showed him the door.

Contrast this to another supplier that I have always considered a partner, Houston, TX-based World Cinema. In the hotel business, we don't (and shouldn't have to) know much about television and satellite technology. That is why it is important to have a supplier that knows it all and that you can trust and rely upon at all times. Clinton Fox and Nancy Beauchamp of World Cinema are such people and I have always considered them as family and just another extension of our business. Over the years, they have saved the day on many emergency situations. They go above and beyond the call of duty and offer suggestions and solutions, knowing that it is the long-term relationship that counts.

Like customers, clients and co-workers, treating suppliers with respect, sharing information and expertise pays off. Partners enjoy trust and a shared vision of the future. Regardless of industry, developing win-win partnerships leads to creating high quality, world-class services and products.

Chapter 5 - Eliminate "Kinks in the Hose"

"The best way to adapt to change is to be the one who's changing things."
- Jeff Tomchik, Manager of Learning Technologies, CVS/Pharmacy

Lance Savage, a friend and also highly regarded hotel revenue management expert, recently reminded me of two (2) very important sayings that have a direct correlation to achieving success in terms of running a quality driven organization...

1. Time is precious. You can't own it, but you can use it. You can't keep it, but you can spend it. Once you've lost it, you can never get it back.

2. There are only two rules. Rule One: The rules keep changing. Rule Two: The only rule that doesn't change is rule one.

Lance is right. Running a high quality business means efficient use of both time and resources, as well as embracing and effectively managing change. Changes in technology have propelled us into a new era of information processing and we must stay ahead of the curve to be successful. As Bill Gates, co-founder of Microsoft Corporation, once stated, *"How you gather, manage, and use information will determine whether you win or lose."*

Years ago, when I first started out in the hotel business, quality was frequently measured by unannounced quarterly quality assurance visits. Inspectors would suddenly pull up to a hotel, and within a matter of hours, check some guest rooms and give the facility and management a score that would be the assessment of quality for that 13 week period.

19

While the quality inspection process of the early 1980's seemed pretty simple and standardized throughout the industry, it also was inherently flawed. First, some managers tracked every movement of the inspectors so that they could determine the approximate time and date that their hotel would be evaluated. This would allow them to literally sweep the dust under the rug and obtain a score that wouldn't accurately reflect the facility. Also, taking a three hour snapshot of a business is certainly not a true indicator of quality over a much longer (3 month) time span.

So, change happened and many hotel companies began to take lessons from other industries, such as manufacturing. The money that was being spent on inspectors traveling throughout the United States was channeled to develop systems that placed the accountability for quality on the front-line team members. For instance, through proper training, the last housekeeper to clean a hotel guest room would be the one responsible for making certain that the room was spotlessly clean with everything in working order.

No matter what field that you are in, reducing cycle time by quickly implementing change is critical to coming out on top of the competition. Information flow must be uninterrupted and immediate. The degree with which an organization is able to allow this to occur will determine who will thrive and/or who will eventually fail.

Throughout my career in the lodging industry, I have learned from many different leaders and people of influence. In the mid-1990's, one of these individuals was Tom Higgins. Tom is now the President and Chief Executive of Best Western International, the world's largest hotel chain with over 4,000 independently owned and operated hotels. A lofty position, yet reflective of Tom's commitment to total quality.

Back in the mid-1990's when I had the opportunity to work with Tom Higgins, we were working for La Quinta Inns. Through Tom's leadership, the company was successful in the nationwide renovation of 225 existing hotels while also developing a new Inn & Suites prototype and expanding. Managing such change would seem difficult, yet as I reflect back on our days together it was surprisingly easy.

You see, Tom insisted on immediate communication flow and making certain that everyone impacted by any change fully understood their role and responsibilities throughout the process. I still remember sitting at a meeting that he held and looking at the centerpieces that adorned each table where we sat. In the middle of each centerpiece, surrounded by beautiful flowers, was a section of garden hose that was all kinked-up. You know, kinked...like when you try to water your yard and turn the spigot on but little or no water comes out of the sprinkler because the hose is twisted. Little did I know at the time that eliminating any "kinks in the hose" would have such an impact on my life and future success.

The centerpieces at this meeting were reflective of the need for uninterrupted and immediate communication flow. With changes happening at an increasingly rapid pace, we could not have any "kinks in the hose". It was our responsibility to make certain that the vision and guidance that Tom provided directly to us was 100% passed along to the front-line team members that were responsible for dealing directly with the customers.

Eliminating all "kinks in the hose" is essential to effectively managing the precious time that we have to implement change. I suggest that you explore your business and see if you find any twisted hose that might exist. Then, remove the kinks and enable maximum saturation to begin.

Chapter 6 - Consistency Counts

"All we're doing is carrying out the ABCs of trucking. You pick it up, deliver it and hope that you don't have a wreck. You don't have to be a genius. You do have to be damned disciplined."

-Russell A. Gerdin, Founder, President & CEO of Heartland Express, Inc.

Over the past decade, I have traveled extensively. In fact, during this time, I have visited hundreds of cities in 37 of the 50 United States of America. During these trips, I have learned many things and have discovered that the following three (3) *absolute truths* are universal in their existence...

1. A taco is the exact same in every Taco Bell restaurant.

2. Taco Bell restaurants are as consistent as their tacos.

3. Taco Bell restaurants do not have tablecloths.

Amazing, yet true. And, you know what? It is no accident. You see, Taco Bell management understands the value of standardized operating procedures and serves up a consistent product that the consumer both understands and expects to be tasty, inexpensive and delivered quickly.

Over the years, Taco Bell restaurants have been through many changes designed to create this consistency and provide a high quality, excellent product. Reducing kitchen sizes, and making it easier to quickly produce all menu offerings, has allowed Taco Bell to grow and prosper while other fast-food companies have become stagnant. Taco Bell customers don't expect tablecloths, nor do they get them. What they do find is an affordable, well-known menu, served at lightning speed.

Another company that values consistency and has been keeping their eye on the ball is AirTran Airways. While most big airlines cut flights and lost billions of dollars in 2002, AirTran posted a $10.7 million profit. How does AirTran continue to grow and be profitable when so many other airlines face economic troubles? Joe Leonard, Chairman and CEO explains, *"I believe it is simply the fact that we hold steadfast to a very simple strategy: Deliver low fares on every seat, on every flight, even for last minute travel. It has become almost a mantra. And because of that, we're earning the trust and loyalty of savvy customers everywhere."*

AirTran is committed to a single mission of *"Delivering the best flying experience to smart travelers."* They succeed by consistently focusing on their guiding principles relating to safety, courtesy, pride, teamwork and innovation. AirTran also maintains one of the very youngest fleet of planes in the industry. By doing so, it costs them 8 percent less to fly and maintain their jets than other airlines that fly the older planes.

In the hotel business, as in these other industries, one must be constantly aware that any variety comes at an additional expense. Maintaining discipline, and resisting the natural inclination of being all things to all people, is critical to success. Learning from the successes of Taco Bell and AirTran Airways can be useful. Whatever you say that you do, do it with excellence. But, don't try to be everything to everybody. It makes no sense, to spend time and money, doing something that you shouldn't be doing in the first place.

Let me give you an example of just how easy it is to lose proper focus. Years ago, I was managing a limited-feature hotel running at very high occupancy. Inside this hotel, we had several rooms that could double either as a guest sleeping room or as a meeting room. I liked the idea of selling these rooms as meeting rooms, because it sort-of made me feel more important. You know, like a full-service hotel operator.

These meeting rooms became very popular. Of course, they were also less expensive than traditional hotel meeting rooms because we didn't offer all the bells and whistles that they did. Still, people expected the room set-up on time and the coffee to be ready upon arrival. With a limited staff, due to the overall nature of the hotel, I often ended up doing the catering, set-up and clean-up duties myself. Eventually, we became so good at the meeting room business, I was ready to convert more guest rooms to having meeting room capability.

That is when I realized, selling meeting rooms at a limited-feature hotel is an obstacle to achieving the true mission of the business (in this case, selling as many sleeping rooms as possible). If a company needed sleeping rooms, plus a place to gather, the meeting rooms were valuable. Yet, if someone wanted to hold a meeting without any sleeping rooms, it was a distraction and not a particularly worthwhile endeavor.

Regardless of what product or service that an organization provides, maintaining zero-defect uniformity is paramount to success. Concentrate on what is truly important to the customer. Sweat the details, and remember that variety kills efficiency. Deliver what you say that you will. Do it with excellence. Channel your energy into what separates you from the rest of the pack. And most of all, remember...*consistency counts!*

II. Service

"Since you get more joy out of giving joy to others, you should put a good deal into the happiness that you are able to give."
-Eleanor Roosevelt, 1884-1962, American First Lady

"Always do more than is required of you."
-George S. Patton, Jr., 1885-1945, General, U.S. Army

"Everybody can be great...because anybody can serve. You don't have to have a college degree to serve. You don't have to make your subject and verb agree to serve. You only need a heart full of grace. A soul generated by love."
-Dr. Martin Luther King, Jr., 1929-1968, Civil Rights Leader

"In the time we have it is surely our duty to do all the good we can to all the people we can in all the ways we can."
-William Barclay, 1907-1978, Scottish Theologian

"Great things are not done by impulse, but by a series of small things brought together."
-Vincent Van Gogh, 1853-1890, Dutch Painter

Chapter 7 - Levels of Customer Service

"There is no higher religion than human service. To work for the common good is the greatest religion."
-Albert Schweitzer, 1875-1965, Nobel Prize Recipient, Humanitarian

Years ago, I was speaking with a group made up of some of the best hotel managers gathered from around the United States of America. During this conference, I asked them all the question, *"What is the most dangerous level of customer service that we can offer?"* To make it simpler, I gave the following three choices...go ahead, what is your answer?

1. *OUTSTANDING SERVICE.* This is when everything is a WOW. In the hotel business, you know when you give this type of service because of the smiles and rave reviews that accompany it. *Fantastic, incredible* and *memorable* are all words that guests use to describe this level of service.

2. *ADEQUATE SERVICE.* This level of service is a wide spectrum ranging between *above average, average,* and *below average.* It is *"Okay".* Not bad, pretty much what one might expect. *Tolerable* is a common descriptor.

3. *UNACCEPTABLE SERVICE.* This is when you are frustrated to the point of taking action. Have you ever asked to speak to a manager? Sent your food back to the kitchen? Asked to have a different hotel room? Things are so bad that you cannot just sit back and do nothing...you *must* let someone know how wrongly that you have been treated.

So, of these three choices, which is the *most dangerous level of service* that one can offer a guest, customer or client? Which do you think, and why? Let me give you a hint...

A Letter From a Nice Customer

"I'm a nice customer. You all know me. I'm the one who never complains, no matter what kind of service I get.

I'll go into a restaurant and sit quietly while the waiters and waitresses gossip and never bother to ask if anyone has taken my order. Sometimes a party that comes in after I did gets their order first, but I don't complain. I just wait.

And when I go to a store to buy something, I don't throw my weight around. I try to be thoughtful of the other person. If a snooty salesperson gets upset because I want to look at several things before making up my mind, I'm just as polite as I can be. I don't believe rudeness in return is the answer.

"The other day I stopped at a full service gas station and waited for almost five minutes before the attendant took care of me. And when he did, he spilled gas and wiped the windshield with an oily rag. But did I complain about the service? Of course, not.

I never kick. I never nag. I never criticize. And, I wouldn't dream about making a scene in public places. I think that is uncalled for. No, I'm the nice customer. And I'll tell you who else I am. I am the customer who never comes back."

-Author Unknown (But Nice)

About twenty years ago I was given this letter and I never have forgotten it. You see, "nice customers" live in that most dangerous level of service called *adequate*. Many businesses spend a ton of money with sales people out trying to bring in a new customer, but fail to create loyalty in already existing clients who might defect to the competition sight unseen.

To give you an example of how dangerous it can be to offer *adequate* service, let me share a story of when I was a *nice* customer taking a large group of hotel trainees out to lunch at a rather well-known, mid-priced restaurant chain.

We had made advance reservations (because time was important), yet upon our arrival we were seated at a table that was much smaller than we had initially requested. No alternative was offered, so we squeezed into our tiny space. Our waiter arrived and it was clear that he "had all the lights on, but nobody was home". He was unable to answer our questions concerning the menu, so we just ordered anyway.

We waited, and waited, and waited for the food to arrive. As we looked for assistance, we noticed that although the manager of the restaurant was visible, he walked around and around never making eye contact with any of the patrons. Incredibly busy, doing nothing. After an hour, the food arrived. Our orders were all mixed up, but we didn't have the time to complain. Instead, we ate, paid the bill and left.

As we exited the restaurant, the manager opened the big, heavy door and said, "Was everything okay?" In a hurry, I answered, "Fine" and gave him *one-handed applause* as I waved "good-bye" to him and his restaurant, *forever*. Funny thing, at the time I was in charge of arranging luncheons for a great number of people on a regular basis. This brief encounter would end up costing this business several thousand dollars in future revenue.

Being in multi-property management for many years, I also know that eventually corporate management would notice that this restaurant's profits were shrinking and a guy like me would start asking why. I can just hear this manager replying, *"I don't know, the guests all say things are FINE."*

Okay, my experience tells me that some of you may have selected *outstanding* as being the most dangerous level of service that one can offer. People typically pick this for one of two reasons...they either think it is a trick question (no), or they make the point that once you reach this incredibly high level of service, the customer's expectations become so high that it is extremely difficult to consistently exceed them.

The answer as to why this doesn't have to be dangerous can be summed up by a couple of examples of organizations known by virtually everyone to be the best in providing consistently outstanding service, *Singapore Airlines* and *Nordstrom's* retail stores. In both cases, people expect 110% service levels, so the key is putting systems in place to achieve *over* 110%.

At Singapore Airlines, Senior Vice President Mr. Sim Kay Wee once explained their success in staying on top for so many years and how their going forward plan to keep the lead while other airlines work hard to mirror their success. *"This is the challenge of being #1,"* Mr. Kim said. *"If you are in the lead and want to stay there, 100% is not enough. You need every member of the team to give 120%."*

Closer to home, Nordstrom is generally recognized as the #1 provider of legendary service in the retail field. It is tough to be the best and when you are, people are constantly looking for you to mess up. In fact, I personally visited a Nordstrom store near Chicago, Illinois just to see if once a business had such an outstanding reputation, how they could continue to exceed already high customer expectations.

As I entered my first Nordstrom experience, I noticed several things. The aisles were unusually open and spacious, the employees were extremely well dressed and polite, and the prices were much higher than the places I usually had shopped. Still, where was the WOW? I decided to first look in the Men's Department where a wonderful gentleman helped me pick out the most expensive tie that I had ever purchased. As he rang up the sale, he told me that Nordstrom was the best place he had ever worked. He said that every day when he walked through the *employee entrance* he was greeted with a sign that said, *"The nicest people in the world pass through these doors."*

Even though that was pretty good, the real WOW was literally just around the corner. As I continued walking through the store, I came upon a piano player entertaining several people. I had seen that before at other stores in the holiday season. However, I had never experienced what I saw next. The piano player suddenly rose from his bench, in his fine tuxedo, walked over to a little girl who was with her mother and asked if she would like to play. She said that she didn't know how. The pianist took the girl's hand, led her to one side of the bench and showed her a few notes to play. They then, together, played the most elegant theme from Disney's *Beauty and the Beast* that I have ever heard. WOW...just imagine the conversation at their home dinner table that night! Nordstrom consistently creates *memories*.

Finally, I suspect that there were more than a few readers that might have chosen *unacceptable* service as being the most dangerous. After all, one could easily reason that if it was that bad, it must be the most dangerous...right? Wrong. The thing about unacceptable service is that it is so bad, the customer will let you know and you will have the opportunity to fix it. You can turn a woe into a WOW! A well handled problem usually creates more loyalty than if the problem never happened in the first place. Together, we will explore putting recovery systems in place to *make it happen.*

Chapter 8 - Are You Listening?

*"I thought we were going to be together forever, and then...
out of the blue she sends me a 'Dear John' letter...she gave
me a bunch of crap about me not listening to her enough, or
something. I don't know, I wasn't really paying attention."*
-Harry Dunn (Actor Jeff Daniels) in the movie, *"Dumb & Dumber"*

Once people understand that offering an adequate level of
service is the most dangerous, the next question I usually
receive is, *"Since, I don't want 'nice' customers to leave and
never come back, how do I measure this and know for sure
exactly what level of service my customers think that our
company has provided to them?"*

The answer is that there are a LOT of ways to receive
feedback in order to measure both customer service and
customer loyalty. During the past twenty years in the
hospitality industry I have seen everything used from the
basic guest comment card to mystery shoppers and focus
groups in an effort to gain the elusive answer to this all-
important question. Some companies worry that the results
are skewed, and even manipulated, depending the way the
questions are asked and the responses interpreted. It can get
unbelievably expensive as one searches for the absolute
truth.

My recommendation...just *ask* the guests, customers
and/or clients about what you are doing best and what can be
improved upon. Huh? It can't be that simple, can it? Yes, it
can; provided that once you *ask*, that you then *listen*. And
once you have effectively listened, there must be a system in
place to get the feedback communicated throughout the
organization so that it can be used to evaluate and determine
future service and product enhancement initiatives.

Let me further explain what I mean about asking what you are doing best and what can be improved upon. This is extremely important. Many people get mixed-up, lose focus of the big picture and unnecessarily spend TONS of money trying to figure out how to just ask. Worse, after finally getting answers, the information is often worthless since it is diluted when it is compiled together and averaged out.

Here is an example of what *not* to do. Have you bought a new car lately? Over the past five years I have bought several new cars for my family and you can tell the importance of the customer feedback surveys to the big car companies. Now, while I believe in the *"I want to be a 10"* concept, the pressure for results has led some dealerships to worry more about the score, than the process. They tell you that you will get a survey and virtually make you swear to the almighty that you will give them an *excellent* rating, no matter what you really think. Instead of *"I want to be a 10"*, it is *"I want you to score me a 10, and don't really care what you think."* Placing the emphasis on something for the wrong reason reminds me of an extended service warranty that was offered to my wife by one car dealership. After we agreed upon the new car price we received a sales pitch for a $500 extended warranty. When we declined, our sales person offered to lower the purchase price of the car by $1,000, *if* we bought the $500 warranty. His sole mission was to sell the warranty, and he gave us $500 to "buy" one.

No, what I am describing when I recommend just asking and listening to people evaluating your service is much simpler, less expensive and there is no reason to manipulate the data. Through this process you will not only learn what you are doing best, better yet, any *"nice"* customers with questionable loyalty will be detected so that recovery measures can be taken.

Again, let me refer back to the hotel business. Just about everyone has stayed in a hotel and upon check-out has heard the desk clerk ask, *"Was everything okay?"* The typical answer is *"fine"*, the guest walks away and nobody has learned anything. Really, it is pretty much the same thing at restaurants, department stores, grocery stores, doctor's offices...everywhere. Even at home when I ask my daughter how her school day was, she replies, *"Fine"*. To really listen, and learn, it takes at least *one more question.*

Getting back to the hotel check-out scenario, if there is nobody else in the lobby within earshot of the conversation, the follow-up question is, *"I am glad things seemed okay. We really want to be the best hotel value in the area, is there anything that you would like me to pass along to top management as to how we might improve in the future?"* The best part of this question is that you will learn if there was anything that might have been disappointing to the guest, so you then can go into recovery mode. Again, this question is only recommended when nobody else is around. I heard one desk clerk ask it in a crowded lobby and it took awhile to diffuse the near-riot as everyone decided to chime in about the closure of the swimming pool on a hot day. Careful!

The alternative question when there are others that will overhear the conversation is, *"I am glad that things were fine, our managers will be pleased that you enjoyed your stay. Is there anything or anyone that you really liked best during your stay with us?"* By asking someone what they liked best, you focus them on positive thoughts as they conclude their final transaction with you. It increases loyalty and reminds them of what they like and why they should come back. In addition, the beauty of asking this one in a crowded lobby allows you to turn a "fine" response into positive word of mouth advertising from a satisfied patron.

Chapter 9 - Turning Woe Into WOW!

"When written in Chinese, the word 'crisis' is composed of two characters - one represents danger and the other represents opportunity."
John F. Kennedy, 1917-1963, 35th President of the United Stares of America

"Stuff" happens. Mistakes are inevitable and despite one's best effort to meet and/or exceed the expectations of each and every person, there will be an occasional *crisis* when a customer or fellow team member becomes less than satisfied. How these *opportunities* are handled determines who will be successful and who will fail.

While the old adage, *"You never get a second chance to make a first impression,"* might often be true, it really doesn't have to be so. Research shows that while 91 percent of those who complain won't come back, you will get 82-95 percent of these customers back if you fix the situation. Better yet, a well handled problem usually creates more loyalty than if the problem never happened in the first place. If you can immediately turn a woe into a WOW, you will create positive word-of-mouth advertising, instead of allowing someone to leave dissatisfied and, on-average, telling nine to ten others about their unhappiness!

Before I share some sure-fire methods of service recovery, let's get a nasty subject out of the way...the *cheaters*. Yes, there are a few people who might try to take advantage of a business or organization by either making something up or over-embellishing a negative situation for personal gain. What should we do about a person trying to take advantage of a situation? Forget about them. That is right; forget about them...for two very good reasons.

The first reason why cheaters are irrelevant is...*that is what hell is for.* You and I don't have to worry about deciding who is right and who is wrong, because in the very end we all are judged by our actions. Those who deliberately lie or stretch the truth will eventually get what is coming to them, plain and simple.

The second reason is equally important...*profitability.* No business or organization can afford to become so judgmental that each person expressing concern might be met with initial skepticism. It is not worth offending (and potentially losing) the 999 out of 1000 customers who are honest and law-abiding to potentially find and capture one cheater.

Instead of being judgmental, the first key to service recovery is to follow these two simple rules whenever dealing with a *moment-of-truth* customer complaint.

RULE #1 - The customer is always right.

RULE #2 - When the customer is wrong, refer to rule #1.

Since it isn't important who is right and who is wrong, the second key to service recovery is to *listen.* Make eye contact with the individual and let them know that you care about what is being explained. Don't interrupt and do take written notes to make certain that you fully understand the situation before doing anything else.

Now that you know that the guest's *perception* is absolute truth and you have listened closely, the third key to service recovery is to *apologize.* By apologizing, make sure to take total responsibility no matter what has happened. Be empathetic as you attempt to clarify the problem and/or develop the solution.

Once you have apologized, the final key to effective service recovery is to *fix the problem* in such a manner that exceeds expectations and leaves the customer saying, *"WOW!"* Having a system in place to accomplish this means having stated guidelines and sufficient training of all team members in regards to specific levels of authority and performance expectations.

One company to benchmark service recovery systems is *The Ritz-Carlton Hotel Company*, a two-time recipient of the Malcolm Baldrige National Quality Award. At Ritz-Carlton, any of the 17,000 employees - known as *"The Ladies and Gentlemen of The Ritz-Carlton"* - can spend up to $2,000 to immediately correct a problem or recover from a complaint. First year managers and employees receive a minimum 250 hours of training, including daily five minute briefings at the start of every shift.

Ritz-Carlton is detailed oriented and all key processes have been dissected to identify points at which errors may occur. For example, to meet its goals of total elimination of problems and 100 percent customer loyalty, they have determined that there are 970 potential instances for a problem to arise during interactions with overnight guests. All employees then receive training reinforcing performance expectations and protocol for interacting with guests and responding to their needs.

Allowing all team members to deal with situations of *crisis* and *opportunity* is an essential winning strategy for any business that deals with people. The customer's perception is always right and your reality. Once this is understood, then simply *listen, apologize,* and *fix the problem* in a fine manner...turning any woe into an unexpected *"WOW!"*

Chapter 10 - Surprising & Delighting Customers

*"I used to think that anyone doing anything weird was weird.
I suddenly realized that anyone doing anything weird wasn't
weird at all and that it was the people saying that they were
weird that were really weird."*
-Paul McCartney, Musician, Songwriter and former member of *"The Beatles"*

The hotel business really isn't about making beds, vacuuming floors and checking people in and out of the guest rooms. No, the hotel business is like most other businesses. It is all about making memories. For, when all is said and done and the credit card bill comes in the mail, it is the memory of the experience that the customer has. If you have succeeded in making fond memories, you will have built a loyal client who will look forward to purchasing from you again and again.

So, how do you make memories? Easy. Simply put a system in place where you are bound to surprise and delight customers. Consider it a proactive approach to ensuring that your business will exceed expectations, and create compelling word-of-mouth advertising as outstanding stories are told and retold to countless prospective future customers.

Quite a few years ago, I asked a diverse group of front-line hotel team members how they made memories for the guests which they served on a daily basis. One enlightened housekeeper said, *"The key is to realize that you aren't just cleaning a bathtub or scrubbing a floor, instead you are making sure that a guest has an overall wonderful experience."* This reminded me of an age-old story of the two stonecutters that were once asked what they were doing. The first said, *"I'm cutting stone into blocks."* The second replied, *"I'm part of a team that's building a cathedral."*

As we continued our discussion relating to memory making, a maintenance engineer expressed that he always made sure to break away from whatever routine duty he might be performing, such as fixing an electrical outlet, to greet or assist a guest with luggage, directions or whatever else they may need. *"After all, it is the customer that is most important, and our future success is completely based on our collective abilities to leave them with a great, everlasting impression of our service,"* he said.

The people attending this meeting really understood the importance of surprising and delighting customers. They were definitely into "WOW" mode. That is when another housekeeper pointed out that she always did something extra-special that would be remembered. An example of this was that she had a box of small dog treats on her housekeeping cart for any guests with a small pet. Paul Forman, a regional hotel manager who was attending the meeting, quickly pointed out, *"That's not just a WOW, that is a BOW-WOW!"* Too funny! Yet, a good question to ask yourself right now is, *"What system does your company or organization have to ensure that memories are made?"* In other words, do you have any "BOW-WOW" in your workplace?

Now, most memory making systems don't revolve around dog treats. What is important is that they appear personalized and random to the customer, thus creating a memorable event that will surprise and delight. For instance, years ago I was in process of relocating from Fort Worth to Atlanta and stayed alone at a Sierra Suites hotel for two consecutive months. My wife, daughter and dog were still back in Texas waiting for the former house to be sold. It was a lonely experience and I only had a stack of their photos with me to look at each night. Housekeeping was only a twice-weekly service at this establishment, but it was memorable. You see, each time I would return home to the hotel at night, the housekeeper had moved the photos. One day they were spread out on top of the bed pillows, another all over the refrigerator, and so on. I no longer felt alone. This wonderful team member obviously recognized my situation by her actions, and I recognized her special caring with a generous tip left at the time of my eventual departure.

The Disney Company is a good example of an organization that understands the importance of making memories. A couple of years ago, while on vacation, we stayed at one of the Disney World Resorts in Orlando, Florida. Our housekeeper was a magician with both bath and hand towels and would make sure to turn one each day into either a bunny rabbit, a swan, a dog or a monkey. We looked so forward to seeing her creations. The towels were nice and thick, too. In fact, the towels were so terrific, we really had trouble closing our suitcases when it was time to leave. Another ever-lasting memory!

Southwest Airlines is another company which knows how to create an environment that surprises and delights customers. When you fly Southwest, you know that you will arrive at your destination safely. Yet, you really never know what fun and surprises are going to happen next. While some airlines give out plastic gold wings to children who are flying, at Southwest, that is just where the games begin. The plane is late, how about a paper-airplane contest in the gate area, with the winner getting a free roundtrip ticket for the future? The plane is delayed departing, how about grabbing two rolls of toilet paper and tee-peeing the entire inside of the cabin - with the two lucky recipients of the cardboard spindles getting special prizes? No matter what line of business you are in, there are many memory making opportunities. Go ahead, don't be afraid, *surprise* and *delight* your customers!

Chapter 11 - A First Time Customer

"If we did all the things we are capable of doing, we would literally astound ourselves."
-Thomas Alva Edison, 1847-1931, U.S. Inventor, Scientist

Take a moment and think about the last time that you entered a business for the very first time. You know, like the first time that you went to a new doctor. Perhaps the first time that you tried out a new restaurant, hotel, retail store, movie theatre or bowling alley. Now, try to remember exactly what you were thinking as you walked into this establishment. Did you feel any anticipation? How about apprehension? More importantly, what were your thoughts as you walked out after this first encounter was concluded?

If you are like most people, there are numerous emotions present whenever something is experienced for the very first time. *A first time customer* is less likely to feel at ease in a new environment than someone who frequents a business on a regular basis. A newcomer usually has questions; the first one being, *"Do I feel comfortable in this place?"* The final question usually is, *"Will I ever come back here again?"*

Most organizations spend a significant portion of their advertising and marketing dollars on efforts that are designed to lure and attract new customers away from the competition. The theory is that a high percentage of these new patrons will continue to shop or revisit the place of business once they are familiar with it. Yet, few companies have a specific plan to ensure that these first time customers are greeted with a warm welcome and receive special VIP treatment so that they will come back, again and again.

Now, some people might question whether it is wise to give first time customers specialized treatment. After all, there is a logical argument to be made that all patrons should be treated as VIPs, right? For the answer to this, go back to when you first rode a bicycle. Didn't someone watch over you closely until you were able to fly solo? How about when you rented your first apartment? Didn't someone answer all the questions you had in great detail, just to make sure that you felt comfortable and understood everything? While everyone should receive excellent service, there is no doubt that a first time customer deserves extra attention.

Referring back to the hospitality industry, every day, in virtually every hotel and restaurant nationwide, an opportunity to serve a first time guest occurs. How these moments-of-truth are handled weighs heavily on whether the business will succeed or whether it will fail. That is why I recommend establishing a system that specifically targets the service given to a first time customer.

Let me give you a detailed example of what such a system might look like. Imagine a first time guest, "Ms. Jones," with a reservation at a hotel that is unfamiliar to her. Let's say the hotel is named, "The Burdakin Inn". Now, as Ms. Jones enters the property for the first time, she really doesn't know what to expect. Is the hotel similar to a "Ritz-Carlton", or is it more like "The Bates Motel" - from *"Psycho"* movie fame?

While Ms. Jones travels through the entrance door and reaches the registration desk, impressions are already being formed. As the hotel representative greets Ms. Jones, he asks, *"Welcome Ms. Jones, have you ever stayed with us before?"* This is a common question that almost every hotelier will ask at the time of check-in. It is the first ingredient of a specific plan to identify a first time customer.

Once Ms. Jones acknowledges that this is her first time staying at the Burdakin Inn, the front desk team member leaps into a detailed explanation of all the services and amenities that the facility has to offer. As he does so, he also makes an inconspicuous notation (for the sake of simplicity, let's say the mark of a /) on the registration card. All team members of the hotel understand this / to mean that Ms. Jones is a first time guest - the second component of the plan.

After Ms. Jones settles into her room, approximately 15 minutes after check-in, the phone rings. *"Hi, Ms. Jones! This is Dan at the front desk and since this is your first time staying at the Burdakin Inn, I just wanted to check and make sure that everything is to your satisfaction and/or answer any additional questions that you might have."* Once this courtesy call is completed, the notation on the registration card is changed from / to X. Once again, all team members know that an X means that a follow-up courtesy call was successfully made to Ms. Jones - the third part of the plan.

As Ms. Jones continues her stay, everyone knows that she is a first time guest and that first time guests are the most vulnerable to leave and never come back. Every interaction, from housekeeping to room-service, takes place with this knowledge. Finally, at check-out, the front desk cashier says, *"Good morning, Ms. Jones. I see this was your first time with us at the Burdakin Inn, how did you enjoy your stay?"* By again using her name, and letting her know that the hotel remembered what she had said at check-in, Ms. Jones now feels welcome and will most likely return.

That is it. Pretty simple. And, every business that deals with people is capable of establishing a similar system to make certain that first time customers have their expectations exceeded. Think about it. What is your system?

Chapter 12 - More Service Tips

*"The moment one definitely commits oneself, then
providence moves too. Whatever you can do or dream you
can, begin it. Boldness has genius, power and magic in it.
Begin it now!"*
-Johann Wolfgang von Goethe, 1749-1832, German Poet, Novelist, Philosopher

At the core of any great service organization are systems.
These systems are specifically designed plans to surprise and
delight customers, turn any woe into a WOW (via
extraordinary service recovery), and to increase loyalty by
making a memorable experience of every customer
encounter. Achieving excellence in the key result area of
service can be difficult, yet it is essential to any successful
business enterprise that deals with people.

Over the years, I have come to realize that there are a
number of additional common elements found in companies
which are leaders in terms of service. These prevalent traits
are important to review and include as your business
develops its own service plan. As you incorporate these
ideas, you will also gain the upper hand and triumph over
your competition. Here are some general service tips that
will help you in this endeavor...

1. Prepare to Win.

In the sporting arena, individuals and teams always
attempt to gain as much information as possible about their
opponent, prior to the match-up. By scouting and studying
the opposition, you learn both their strengths and weaknesses
and discover how you can get an edge. When I was growing
up, it was Ali v. Frazier, Nicklaus v. Palmer, and Magic v.
Bird. In each case, these superstars prepared well in advance

of the game being played. The same applies to your business. Knowing how the competition will react in certain situations helps you develop your own game plan and strategies.

Preparation for outstanding service also involves training and making certain that all the supplies needed are readily available to the front-line team members. Problems can only be handled quickly if everyone knows exactly what their limitations are, and if the necessary tools are available at all times. Look around, does your company enable quick service delivery by removing all obstacles to success?

2. Make it Personal.

This can be tricky, because while we talk about establishing systems, some people get mixed up and develop processes that are so rigid that the personalized touch is removed. For instance, in the hotel business, I have seen "Guest of the Day" programs. While the idea of keeping the team members focused on at least one daily WOW is brilliant, this can lose its luster if not implemented correctly. Placing a sign in the lobby announcing the "Guest of the Day" means that one person wins, while all the other guests lose. Also, it is seen as a "program", instead of a WOW. Rather, it would be wise to just put a handwritten note and surprise in the recipient's room. In fact, if you follow this strategy, you can have many "Guests of the Day" on the same day.

Smile at your customers and use their names whenever you can. Remember special things about them so that you can bring them up in future conversations. Where a person is from and whether they have children, pets or hobbies are all topics that people like to talk about. And I'll say it again, use names often. It is the sweetest sound to a person's ears.

3. Remove "CAN'T" From Your Vocabulary.

Shari Barber, a friend of mine, once told me, *"Never say that anything CAN'T be done, because CAN'T NEVER COULD!"* She believes that nothing is impossible and if you believe in yourself, all things are possible. She is right.

How things are phrased have a tremendous impact on how your level of service is perceived. For instance, one time I stayed at a moderately priced hotel and called the front desk to see if a hairdryer was available for loan. I was told, *"You will HAVE TO come to the front desk, I CAN'T bring it to your room."* Now, prior to this, the only things that I was aware that I *"have to"* do is pay taxes and die. That aside, it sure would have sounded better to hear that the hotel would be happy to deliver it to my room as soon as housekeeping arrived, and if I needed it sooner recommend that I pick one up at the front desk. Same thing, yet a world of difference.

4. Nobody Leaves Unhappy.

One time, I knew of a lodging company that had 75 hotels, averaging 110 guest rooms at each, running 70% occupancy at a $50 average daily rate. Better yet, this organization ran a particularly high guest satisfaction rating with 97.5% of the guests surveyed stating that they *"will stay again"*.

While this sounds very good, it also points to the value of making certain that every guest leaves happy and will return. This hotel company rents 2,107,875 rooms each year and if 2.5% leave and won't come back, that is 52,696 lost room nights at a $50 average daily rate, or $2,634,843 in lost revenue next year. Worse, if they don't come back in future years, this amount is multiplied over and over again. Every customer counts. Make sure that nobody leaves unhappy.

III.   Teamwork

"Everything is a team. There's no guy you single out for doing this or not doing this. When you do anything as a team, whether you win or lose or make an error, it's the team doing that. And that's the approach you need to have."
-Joe Torre, Manager of the New York Yankees Baseball Team

"People become really quite remarkable when they first start thinking that they can do things. When they really believe in themselves they have the first secret to success."
-Norman Vincent Peale, 1898-1993, Author

"Individual commitment to a group effort--that is what makes a team work, a company work, a society work, a civilization work."
-Vincent T. Lombardi, 1913-1970, Former Coach of the Green Bay Packers

"Good thoughts are no better than good dreams, unless they are executed."
-Ralph Waldo Emerson, 1803-1882, American Poet

The way a team plays as a whole determines its success. You may have the greatest bunch of individual stars in the world, but if they don't play together, the club won't be worth a dime."
-George "Babe" Herman Ruth, 1895-1948, Hall of Fame Baseball Player

Chapter 13 - Creating a Winning Team

"Should you feel your energy lapsing, try this surefire remedy: Find someone who needs a helping hand, a word of support, or a good ear - and MAKE THEIR DAY!"
-Stephen C. Lundin, Ph.D., Author of *"FISH!"*

TEAMWORK is made up of many things, *synergy*, *diversity*, *cooperation* and a *common purpose* - just to mention a few. Yet, I believe that the foundation of teamwork is centered upon its *leadership*. I have seen many great individuals in my life, yet far fewer great teams. What turns an ordinary group of people into a winning team is the coach.

Don Smith, professor and former director of Michigan State University's *"The* School of Hospitality Business" had it right when he taught us, *"The coach makes the difference."* I have been involved in opening 96 different hotels across the United States. Whether it is Portland, San Diego, Houston, Detroit or Miami...inevitably, the hotels that succeeded had managers who would know when to offer rewarding praise to their team members. Here is an example of how this universal truth applies to hotels, golf, baseball teams and just about everything. Positive leadership creates winning teams.

Back in 1993, a work associate and I successfully bid on a charity golf package (benefiting the Mathew Dickey Boys Club) to play golf with baseball manager Joe Torre. At the time, Joe was managing the St. Louis Cardinals. Since then, he led the New York Yankees to the World Series on numerous occasions. The event was to take place at the *Bellerive Country Club* (host to the 74th PGA Golf Tournament the following week), a very challenging course.

Just days before the golf outing, Joe called and asked if we minded if he brought along a couple "friends", former pitching greats Joe Coleman and Bob Forsch. Of course, we agreed and decided that we would have two groups and just switch partners after the first nine holes, so that we each would have the opportunity to play with Joe Torre.

In the morning, as we drove to the golf course, Eric, my friend from work, showed me some old baseball cards for each of them...Joe Torre, Joe Coleman and Bob Forsch. As I looked the cards over, I noticed that on the back of Joe Coleman's, it said, *"In his spare time, Joe is a scratch golfer."* Uh-oh, that means he is very good...at least 25 strokes better than I, but it was too late to pull out!

After the first nine holes, we switched partners and I finally was to play with Joe Torre and Joe Coleman. As we did, Eric and I exchanged words about how we didn't belong playing with these guys because they were so much better than us. Both of us were humiliated and defeated, yet in awe of these baseball legends and still having fun because of them.

On the 10th tee, Joe Coleman hit a smashing drive and Joe Torre followed with another one. It was my turn and I hit the ball about 10 yards into the long rough grass already prepared for the PGA Tournament. I hit the second shot another 10 yards and had now made it past the women's tee box. My third shot showed little improvement and I walked back to Joe Torre, sitting in our golf cart. Ugh. Ugh. Ugh.

I apologized to Joe for my overall incompetence and poor play. He looked at me and said, "Dan, don't worry about us...we are just happy to be here playing and relaxing. You are the VIP here. Your donation to the charity made today possible and you are the important one, not us."

WOW! Believe it or not, on my next shot I hit a 3 iron like never before (or since) and it landed within a few feet of the hole. Talk about the positive power of praising people! No wonder Joe Torre teams consistently win. While he could have been frustrated and/or angered that he was stuck with a weak partner, he chose to make the best of the situation and manage his fellow team member to a higher level. His leadership style of enhancing self-esteem is the key ingredient in bringing out the best in any team.

In the business world, there are countless examples of positive leadership creating winning teams. Herb Kelleher of *Southwest Airlines*, Michael Eisner of *Disney*, Gordon Bethune of *Continental Airlines* and David Glass of *Wal-Mart* are just a few great coaches who have made the difference in their respective organizations.

This same concept is also applicable on the home-front. My daughter, Nicole, is in the sixth-grade and has just begun taking band lessons with her shiny new clarinet. The first day that she brought it home she struggled to make any noise come from the instrument. Each time a "honk" did occur, we showered her with praise. Now, just several weeks later Nicole is playing songs and making beautiful music. Yesterday, when she got home from school I asked her how her day went and she said, *"Fine"*. So I asked her a follow-up question as to what she liked best about her day of learning and she replied, *"Our band leader told us that he was really proud of how well the woodwind section was doing."* I guess her teacher also understands the positive power of praising people. Nice job and thanks, Mr. Bertles!

Chapter 14 - The Magic of a Light Bulb

"Alone we can do so little. Together we can do so much."
-Helen Keller, 1880-1968, Presidential Medal of Freedom Recipient

A few years ago, I observed an interesting moment-of-truth interaction between a guest and a hotel team member. *"Do you have a light bulb?"* the guest inquired of the front desk worker. The hotel employee proudly announced, *"Yes!"* as he handed the guest a light bulb.

Now, something didn't seem quite right about all this because most hotel guests don't have to ask for a light bulb. While the desk clerk silently prayed that this would be the end of their brief encounter, the guest took a few steps down the hallway and then quickly returned to the counter.

"It's a funny thing about this light bulb," the guest announced. *"You see, when I checked in it was late and I went straight to bed and turned on the light to read and the bulb was burned out. I thought perhaps it had just burned out and so I decided that the housekeeper would replace it in the morning. Upon returning from work yesterday, the burned out bulb remained. I figured the housekeeper just hadn't noticed it, so this morning I unscrewed the bulb and left it on the night-stand next to the bed. As I returned to my room this evening, I was relieved to see the housekeeper had removed the old light bulb but then noticed that she had not replaced it. Why do you think she would do such a thing?"*

"Hmmm...I dunno," answered the not-so-sharp hotel representative as the guest then turned and began the long walk back to his room. Poor quality, poor service and then poor teamwork combined for a miserable guest experience.

The energy of light is symbolic of *teamwork*. Alone, it might be just a plain, average bulb with light dispersed in all directions. Yet, focused on a single subject, it can be a laser beam burning through any barrier that might exist.

Now, just imagine how teamwork could have been applied to the guest's light bulb problem and how working together the hotel workers should have concentrated their energy to turn this woe into a WOW!

"Yes, we have plenty of light bulbs and would be happy to replace any that might have burned out. Would you like me to have one of our team members dispatched immediately to your room to ensure that all fixtures are properly functioning?" asks the front desk guest service agent.

"That would be great," responds the guest. *"I left a bulb on the nightstand for the housekeeper to replace, but instead she just removed it. Perhaps there is something wrong with the light."*

Immediately, faster than any hotel employee in the history of the world ever responded, a maintenance engineer meets the guest back in the room. *"I am sorry that you have experienced a problem with the light. We expect everything to be in 100% working order during your stay and anytime we fall short of that goal, please let us know."* As he replaces the bulb and verifies the fixture is fine, he goes on to say, *"Because of your inconvenience, I have also stopped at the hotel gift shop and brought a few snacks that you might enjoy while you read or watch television this evening."*

The next day, the housekeeper leaves a hand-written, personalized note with an apology for any inconvenience that might have been encountered due to not replacing the bulb and the General Manager of the hotel leaves a voice mail inquiring as to how the guest's stay is going, whether the staff has met and/or exceeded expectations and leaving a name with phone number if the guest would like to provide further comments or has any potential referral business for the hotel from co-workers or acquaintances.

Whether it is a hotel, restaurant or any other organization that deals with people, it is imperative that abilities are harnessed and efforts concentrated on a common goal. One company that shines brightly in this area is *Art Cleaners* in Atlanta, Georgia.

Art Cleaners has impeccable quality, same-day cleaning and reasonable prices, but the employees are the ones working together to astound and delight the repeat patrons. Let me explain what it feels like to be a customer of *Art Cleaners*... it reminds me of a NASCAR driver pulling in for a quick pit-stop. At Art Cleaners, customers pull up into the drive-thru lane and are immediately met with a smile and greeting that always includes their name. This is true even if it is busy and there are several cars in-line. No kidding, they actually leave the building and walk to your car and welcome everyone! While one person is accepting new incoming drop-off clothes, another team member is already retrieving pick-up items. Other team members sewing in the back take the time to smile, wave and shout, *"Hello!"* Everyone knows their role and sincerely enjoys working together to provide a terrific and memorable experience. The added surprises like a dog treat for canine passengers, a lollipop for a small child or a bottle of *Martini & Rossi* sparkling wine for the adults on New Year's is just the icing on the cake. Art Cleaners really shines the brightest with their *excellence* in *teamwork.*

Chapter 15 - First Day Attitude

"Start every day as if it was your first day on the job."
-Jack Welch, former Chairman and CEO of General Electric

I was in Indianapolis about ten years ago, trying to figure out why a particular hotel was having a problem with high employee turnover amongst the hourly team members. The hotel was in a nice area, working conditions appeared to be good and yet only one hourly associate remained from the hotel's opening just a few years prior.

Back in the days when I was a property level General Manager, I always made sure to briefly visit with everyone at the beginning of their shift, and also during as many break-times as possible. At the time of this visit, I was a Regional Manager and attempted this same strategy. I waited at the employee breakfast/lunch table early in the morning so that I could say *"Hi"* to everyone as they arrived, and get a feeling of the general mood that existed.

As I sat there, several new team members arrived who I did not know (not surprising, considering that the main issue at this hotel was excessive turnover). I introduced myself and told them how excited we were to have them in our organization and how we were looking forward to a long-term, mutually rewarding relationship. They all seemed excited and enthusiastic. Peter, a housekeeper who was the only original employee left, showed up carrying a newspaper.

As Peter opened the paper, he immediately pulled out the classified advertising "help wanted" section and started announcing to everyone the various alternative opportunities which were available within the community.

As everyone punched-in on the time-clock and began to head for their own assignments, I asked Peter to stay around and talk to me about how things were going. He said that he was very happy, but he was frustrated that he had to train so many new employees. I was relieved to hear that Peter was somewhat satisfied, yet questioned him as to why he was searching the "help-wanted" section of the newspaper. He said, *"I always do that, just to let everyone know what openings the other hotels have in case anyone is interested."*

What Peter didn't realize is something that I have come to find as a common situation at a number of businesses throughout the years. The new employees often get their most important training by watching and learning what the long-term team members do and say, and the attitude that they display. In this case, the lone veteran was scaring away the newcomers who surely were thinking to themselves that if they stayed with us for a few years they, too, could look forward to a career of reading the "help-wanted" advertisements each morning. Inspiring, right?

So, who was at fault in this situation? Peter? The property General Manager? No, it was my responsibility to provide an environment that was stimulating and challenging and communicate each person's role and importance to the organization. The first remedy here was to help Peter understand that he was the most valuable person that we had and that he could help reduce his own frustration by taking a different approach with the new hires.

If Peter was able to communicate how happy and satisfied he really was, perhaps it would have a snow-ball effect on the others and we could begin to build a real team at this location. Peter gave his commitment that he would help become part of the solution to the turnover problem.

Like Peter, the General Manager at this hotel had been similarly frustrated with the constant training and turnover. It seemed like people just wanted to get a few paychecks before leaving for another better-paying job. While that does occasionally happen, I shared my belief that most people are excited and want to be successful when they start work with a new employer. Think about it, remember your enthusiasm on each "first day" of a new job? The following scenario describes the typical employment cycle at an organization struggling with high turnover and low job satisfaction.

A new team member almost always shows up early for their first day of work, clothes pressed and well-groomed. Since there is extra time, they go into the employee restroom to primp for a few minutes. In this restroom, there are a number of discarded paper towels laying on the floor near the trashcan. The new employee doesn't want to see a mess at their wonderful new place of employment, so they pick them up and throw them all away.

A couple weeks go by, and this same employee arrives just a few minutes before work, stops by the same restroom and washes their hands. The individual sees other paper towels laying on the floor but just makes sure to get their own placed into the trash, too busy to pick up after others.

Months later, this particular team member is now tardy for work. While wearing a wrinkled shirt, this person quickly stops by the employee restroom to clean their hands and then tosses the used paper towel onto the floor, next to the others.

The lesson to be learned is that people generally want to do a good job and be proud of their workplace. Management has the responsibility to provide a challenging workplace where all team members can maintain their *first day* attitude.

Chapter 16 - Signs, Signs, Everywhere a Sign...

"I look forward to helping build a company that treasures
the people who work for it."
-Dwight "Ike" Reighard, Chief People Officer, HomeBanc Mortgage

The sign said, *"Employee of the Month Parking Only."* It was located in the best parking spot, nearest to the store, and it seemed like a good sign that management cared about their team members. My wife and I noticed this sign just a little over five years ago when we first moved to Atlanta, Georgia. The store was part of a well-known discount retail chain, based in the Midwest (near our hometown), and we were delighted to find a location so close to our new house.

On our first visit, this prestigious "Employee of the Month" parking spot was unused and left empty. Cheryl and I surmised that the honorary recipient was most likely given the day off with pay as a result of this important designation. We were initially impressed. Yet, as we went inside, our experience became changed from what we had expected. There were very few employees and those that were available seemed uninformed and indifferent. The shelves were poorly stocked and nobody could answer the questions that we had.

Over the course of the next four years, my wife and I continued to patronize this store, in spite of similar and consistent mediocrity. Why? Well, first we had a deep allegiance to the chain/brand with memories from our childhoods growing up in the Midwest. And secondly, we wanted to find out who this mysterious "Employee of the Month" really was. No kidding, every time that either one of us shopped there, we never found a car parked in the finest space with this sign of distinction. Empty. Empty. Empty.

Finally, one day, it all became clear. The reason that the legendary parking spot had remained absolutely unused for so long was that the service and teamwork, at this location, was so horrible that not a single soul in four whole years had qualified to be "Employee of the Month."

Mercifully, approximately six months ago, the once-promising sign was removed and the parking space given back to the paying customers. My wife and I celebrated. Never more would we know, in-advance of entering the store, that nobody had yet received the award . The victory of having the sign come down was short-lived, though. This giant retailer from our home-town soon declared Chapter 11 Bankruptcy. We were saddened by the news because the "sign" of this eventuality had literally been posted for years.

I have seen many bad signs, in my career. While often well-intentioned, bad signs seem to proliferate and sneak into our workplaces and act as a cancer. I am convinced that bad signs can be the death of any team, and eventually any organization that allows them to exist. Think about it.

"NO SHOES, NO SHIRT, NO SERVICE, NO EXCHANGES, NO RETURNS, NO REFUNDS, NO SHOPLIFTING, NO FOOD, NO DRINKS, NO STROLLERS, NO BARE FEET, NO TANK TOPS, OUT OF ORDER, TAKE A NUMBER, RING BELL, NO VACANCY, and *THREE GARMENT LIMIT,"* are all bad signs that consumers are exposed to on a regular basis. You would think that the economy was booming since businesses continue to post such atrocities. It is sad. And, for those of us who often spend time behind the scenes, we know that this is just the tip of the iceberg. The cancer typically begins silently from within and the disease then spreads outward from the inner source.

"CLEAN UP AFTER YOURSELF, EAT ONLY THE FOOD THAT IS YOURS, DO NOT STEAL OTHER PEOPLE'S FOOD, ALL FOOD LEFT AT NIGHT WILL BE THROWN AWAY, KEEP THIS CLEAN, DON'T EAT, DON'T CHEW GUM, NO OVERTIME," are often the warning signs posted in the employee break rooms and/or near time clocks. The signs that the environment is unhealthy. The signs that teamwork is lacking and that doom is likely ahead.

Yes, bad signs are just bad news. Worse yet, if they are handwritten or have "yellowed" over time since their original posting, they can be particularly fatal. IMPORTANT...Any sign posted must be closely inspected. It needs to be professional, of a positive nature and create goodwill. A sign needs to build teamwork or build a customer's loyalty.

Publicly posted "Employee of the Month" signs can be good. Yet, if they aren't maintained they become bad. In one hotel that I visited, the "Employee of the Month" plaque was publicly displayed in the lobby. The only problem was that it only had ten name-plates which fit on the award. With twelve months and only ten slots, this well-intended effort was destined for failure. Management's commitment to the award was obviously lacking, since the funds to get the needed larger plaque had not been allocated.

Team member recognition is VERY important. However, let's also recognize bad signs. Regardless of whatever organization or business that you represent, look around and help stomp-out bad sign pollution. Rip them down! Throw them out! Replace them with positive and professional signs that emphasize or follow your mission or vision statements. Doing so will improve morale and teamwork, in addition to also improving customer satisfaction and revenues, too!

Chapter 17 - Team Member of the Moment!

"What we do at Disney is very simple. We set our goals, aim for perfection, inevitably fall short, try to learn from our mistakes and hope that our successes will continue to outnumber our failures. Above all, we tell stories, in the hope that they will entertain, inform and engage."
-Michael Eisner, Chairman and CEO of The Walt Disney Company

By now, it should be apparent that I am not a huge fan of "Employee of the Month" parking spaces and/or signs. While these tools can be valuable, they also can have a reverse impact and actually demoralize a workforce. Often, employees consider "Employee of the Month" just another political game. Depending on the size of the business, either the same person wins each month, or the other extreme occurs with virtually every employee winning an obligatory month. Assuming that management actually stays on-top of the program and has timely winners, figuring out the criteria and why one person is recognized above the rest is confusing.

That is why I am an advocate of implementing a "Team Member of the Moment" recognition-based program. Huh? That's right, "Team Member of the Moment." Why? Well, for starters, I prefer to call work associates "team members" instead of "employees". A small differentiation, perhaps, yet I view today's business environment as being very competitive and everyone must participate to be a winner. It is all about being a team. Also, why celebrate success only once a month? It is much more effective to tie recognition immediately to any miraculous feat which may occur, without notice, at any time. Like Disney, Nordstrom and Southwest Airlines, this creates a fun-filled workplace, and provides endless legendary story-telling opportunities.

Creating teamwork through a positive work environment that regularly salutes triumphant acts performed by team members reminds me of the "Good News Philosophy" of Randy Hulce, a former boss and mentor of mine. Randy, currently President and Chief Operating Officer of VenQuest Hotel Group, used to regularly ask the question, *"So, what is the good news?"* of both his management and front-line team members. Randy always expected a quick, uplifting response to this question. At any moment, if we had good news to report, he knew that we were really making a difference. Believe me, everyone walked around with a success story on the tip of their tongue whether Randy was around or not. Better to be safe, than sorry. Better to win than to lose.

Tying the concept of "Team Member of the Moment" together with always having a "Good News Philosophy," means having a dynamic workplace where communication, positive attitudes and teamwork reign supreme. It also means that you need to make sure to have a Polaroid instant camera and LOTS of extra film available, because one never knows when a legendary story might be created!

Some people think that only huge accomplishments are the ones that deserve recognition. That is not true. If you look around, there are many random acts of unselfish kindness going on all the time. In my most recent position, I used a program entitled, "The Thought of the Day" to communicate these success stories via e-mail on a daily basis. Some were simply from comment cards, which we would receive at the corporate office, recognizing team members. Others, combined with inspirational quotes, would be tales of outstanding performance with work associates being caught, doing something right. Take for instance, this story of a simple interaction that I had with a hotel Guest Service Agent in March, 2001...

The Pen

Earlier this week, I asked Maria at the Chicago Oak Brook hotel's front desk if I could borrow a pen for my meeting - as I had misplaced several pens previously in my possession. I started to reach for one of the standard stick-type cheapies and then Maria stopped me, went into the back office and brought back a nice Parker pen. The fact that it was a Michigan State dark green color made it that much nicer.

The next day, having thought about the experience, I asked her if it was her own personal pen. She reluctantly affirmed my suspicion. WOW! She was willing to give up her own personal pen so that I would look better than if I were to use the cheap kind at such an important meeting. I'll be sending it back to her, soon with my heartfelt thanks and appreciation for again giving that little "extra" that turns ordinary into extraordinary.

Now, the above tale wasn't anything gargantuan or enormous. Yet, it was a great story worth telling to the entire company. A selfless, good deed executed by someone who wasn't looking for a reward. Nice. I was only too happy to include a handwritten note along with a new, commemorative Cross pen along with her Parker pen when I mailed Maria's writing instrument back to her.

Surprising and delighting outstanding associates, such as Maria, promotes teamwork and recognizes excellence. Better yet, it can instill a positive culture within the workplace, as well as make lifetime memories for deserving individuals. Have you ever received a gold star, a fancy certificate, or a flowery carnation while at work? It feels good, doesn't it? Yes, it feels real good. Now, look around, who is your current "Team Member of the Moment?"

Chapter 18 - Having Fun at Work

"On the starting block before my first Olympic race, I was smiling because I was having fun. That is what it is all about, having fun."
-Janet Evans (American Swimmer, Olympic Gold Medallist)

A few years ago, some fish mongers at a small, humble, unassuming fish stand located in an open-air market in the heart of Seattle, Washington committed themselves to becoming "world famous." They have since accomplished this - not by spending money on advertising (they claim to have never spent a dime), but by being truly great with people, and making happy memories

The fish mongers at *"World Famous Pike Place Fish"* have chosen to interact with people while maintaining a strong desire to make a difference for them. And, it works. People now come from all over the world to see this world famous team throwing fish and having fun with customers. Of course, people also come to buy some of the best seafood available anywhere in the world and have it shipped home.

What makes Pike Place Fish different from any other fish market is that it is just plain *fun*. A good time is assured for both visitors and fish mongers alike. They make certain to give each person the experience of having been served and appreciated, whether a visitor buy any fish or not. The fish mongers truly believe and act with the philosophy that they can improve the quality of life for others and impact the way other people experience life.

I presume that most readers are familiar with Pike Place Fish, as the antics of the fish-flinging staff have been featured on numerous television shows, including NBC's

"Frasier," and ABC's *"Good Morning America."* For those who may not have experienced this "World Famous" and fun environment, I suggest that you visit their website at www.pikeplacefish.com and check out what you have been missing.

The most interesting aspect of Pike Place Fish is that one of the greatest places to work is actually a fish market. Fish stores are cold, damp places that smell like dead fish. If this type of environment can be transformed into a high-energy, fun-filled workplace, surely any other business can learn from the fish mongers and also choose to be "World Famous."

Another unassuming organization that embraces the value of having fun at work is the *Waffle House* restaurant chain. Based in Atlanta, Georgia, there are currently more than 1,300 Waffle House restaurants operating in 24 states. If somehow you are not familiar with a Waffle House restaurant, a brief description would be that of an old Southern roadside diner, open 24-hours per day and featuring quick, friendly service.

Once again, it is difficult to understand how an establishment such as a Waffle House restaurant can be considered a high-energy, fun-filled workplace. Well, it begins with a choice that Waffle House has made with a mission to become *"America's Place to Work and America's Place to Eat."* The associates of Waffle House have decided to always immediately greet customers as they walk in, and then treat everyone like an old friend. On some occasions, these same team members might even launch into one of the classic waffle songs, such as *"Waffle Doo Wop"* or *"Waffle House Family"*, which are found on every Waffle House jukebox.

One more thing about Waffle House. Like Pike Place Fish, they are not only fun and extremely popular, they are also very profitable enterprises. Interestingly, Waffle House is actually the world's leading server of waffles, T-bone steaks, omelets and hash browns, among other items. In-fact, if you stack all of the sausage patties Waffle House sells in just one day, the stack would be as tall as the Empire State Building. The good food, delivered by associates having fun, is why so many celebrities (including singers Britney Spears, LeAnne Rimes and Faith Hill, as well as Former President George Bush) have been seen enjoying dining at *"America's Place to Work and America's Place to Eat"*.

In my years in the hotel business, I have seen many examples of people having fun at work. For instance, one hotel noted that they received a large number of requests for additional pillows. Seizing the opportunity to have fun, the team members respond by taking loads of pillows, all different sizes, immediately to any guest with such an inquiry. So much more fun than just handing over an extra pillow!

Another example of having fun came from a hotel that found it boring just to ask all guests if they wanted to receive a wake-up call. At random, they would select guests needing a smile and ask if they wanted the "regular" wake-up call or the "special". Those adventurous enough to request the "special" would receive a phone call with a rooster crowing, followed by the weather forecast for their hometown city.

Regardless of your profession, having fun is largely just a simple choice that team members make to enjoy each day and cherish the smiles on the faces of customers and co-workers. Holiday decorating contests, parties, and special events are other excuses to create happiness and spice things up. Maintain professionalism, but also keep things fun!

IV. Profitability

"Managing a business, whether it is a large corporation or a small shop, is a daily accumulation of numbers.
- Kazou Inamori, Author of *"A Passion for Success"*

"The people who get on in this world are the people who get up and look for the circumstances they want, and, if they can't find them, make them."
-George Bernard Shaw, 1856-1950, Dramatist

"You always have to keep studying, keep learning, keep discovering how you can get an edge."
-Rick Pitino, Author of *"Success is a Choice"*

"The world is moving so fast these days that the man who says it can't be done is generally interrupted by the man doing it."
-Harry Emerson Fosdick, 1878-1969, American Minister

"Does each decision you make or action you take help in building a tradition of excellence or advancing your core purposes?"
-Jim Potts, Former President & CEO of Homestead Studio Suites Hotels

Chapter 19 - A "Unique" Perspective

Q. *"What is a unique way to catch a wild rabbit?"*

A. *"Unique up on it!"*

Q. *"How do you catch a tame rabbit?"*

A. *"Tame way!"*

(Story told by Charles L. Drury, Sr., Co-Founder of Drury Inns, Inc.)

I know what many of you are thinking. Shouldn't a balance of *Quality, Service & Teamwork* automatically lead to *Profitability*? If the service/profit chain works, the financial rewards will surely follow once excellence is achieved in all the other key operational areas.

While I substantially agree with that position, I think that it is still important to discuss several key concepts in relation to having a highly profitable business. Charles L. Drury, Sr. (CLD) has long been a leader in the private sector of the hotel business. His son, Chuck Drury (President of Drury Inns), has also been one of my many mentors over the years and I want to share what I learned from each of them.

First, I remember when CLD asked the above questions many years ago at a group dinner. As he discussed the answers and I associated them with my many CLD experiences, I came to understand the importance of remaining quietly humble despite any and/or all success that you may encounter. In addition, Chuck displayed that combining this strategy of removing one's ego and replacing it with a second-to-none work ethic provided an unmatchable one-two punch that is a winner in any business endeavor.

Today, Drury Inns owns and operates over 100 locations and consistently is rated by independent research agencies as among the very highest in guest satisfaction. For those who have worked with either CLD and/or his son Chuck, Drury's continued high-level of profitability is really no secret at all.

Most importantly, Drury Inns is a high achiever in all of the key operational areas of *quality, service & teamwork*. Yet, to gain customer base and additional business is even more than that. As CLD said, *"Unique up on it!"*. What this means is that Drury tends to underplay any success achieved. Don't believe for a minute when any Drury team member describes how rough times are and how sad business is. After-all, they certainly don't want to alert any manager at a competitive hotel of any opportunities that might exist with Drury clients.

"Times are tough, please send us any overflow that your business might have," a common quote from many a Drury manager trying a *unique* way to beg for business and catch a new customer. In the meantime, once the opportunity to catch an occasional wild rabbit (or new customer) is realized, look for them to continue the relationship by maintaining their excellence in *quality, service & teamwork.* Tame way.

And don't think that the day ends at 5p.m. for the Drury team. Though President of such a large group of successful hotels, Chuck has been known to visit the competition (hunting for rabbits) at all hours of the night. I have personally seen his extraordinary drive and determination to figure out how to capture more market-share by asking a series of open-ended questions of the overnight/graveyard shift workers at nearby, neighboring hotels. Work harder than the other guy, it pays off. Combining hard work with quiet success, you will sustain profitability and also find that you will have many more good days, than bad.

While I realize that much of this is just common sense, it is amazing how many people let their egos get in the way of their success. In the hotel business, most hotels call each other on a regular basis to determine who has availability and what the competitive rates are. Interestingly, these "call-arounds" frequently have guest service agents and managers *over*stating their true numbers. For whatever misguided reason, they don't want to let the competition know that they are doing poorly.

Let me share an example from August, 1999 in St. Louis. Earlier that summer, we had just opened a brand new hotel in the Westport area and it had never filled despite generally high occupancies in the area. Concerned, I flew into town and spent a couple of days meeting with the management team to determine what we could do to achieve better results.

As I reviewed the call-around reports, I noticed that most hotels in the area were 100% full, while our hotel struggled at about 65%. Listening to the front desk clerks talking with other hotels though, they overstated our status and barely even asked for referrals. Ugh. So, I announced to everyone that we were going to fill that night. I didn't care that it was a Thursday (normally a slower night). We were going to fill. The disbelieving team members laughed as we put a plan in place that those working the desk would call each hotel and announce that we had TONS of rooms left and would have availability all night. Better yet, the managers of our hotel called every other manager at the sold-out competition and told them that our company's Vice President was visiting and was furious that we were so slow while others were full. Begging and pleading for help, the managers communicated desperation. Soon, lines began forming at the check-in counter. Mark McGwire hit his 500th homerun that night, while our team in St. Louis hit their first 100% sell-out, too.

Chapter 20 - Let the Players Know the Score

"Communicate everything you can to your associates. The more they know, the more they care."
-Sam Walton, the late founder of Wal-Mart Stores

The year was 1987 and I had just arrived as General Manager of a hotel located in Corpus Christi, Texas. I didn't know anything about the area, just that the hotel had lost approximately $500,000 in its first year of operation and $600,000 in its second year. The previous management had taken the position that they had done "all they could" and the owners of the hotel couldn't continue to accept the financial bleeding that was occurring, so change was inevitable.

In addition to the huge dollar losses, the hotel also had the most guest complaints in the chain and had failed every quality assurance inspection since it had opened. Clearly, there was no balance in terms of the key areas of quality, service, teamwork & profitability - each was unstable.

Implementing Stephen Covey's principle, *"Seek first to understand, and then to be understood,"* I spent the first couple of nights after my arrival, just sitting in the lobby and watching as an occasional traveler would enter seeking accommodations. Some of the hotel's Guest Service Agents were awful. One spent company-time babysitting her grandchild, and another made frequent trips to the restroom (where a vodka bottle quickly evaporated). Some prospective guests would come in, express surprise at the high room rates and leave - never seeing a room nor getting a sales pitch of all the benefits that were included such as free breakfast and local telephone calls. Complacency and mediocrity reigned. At least this meant opportunities existed.

Unsure of which specific course of action we should take, a mandatory meeting was called with all team members attending. I planned to ask them how they felt things were going and where we could specifically improve our operation. Conducting a meeting like this would seem difficult in a busy hotel environment, but when business is so bad that there are few guests and the phone isn't ringing…it is surprisingly easy.

Well, everyone showed up for the meeting and you can imagine my shock when the entire team's consensus was that *"Our hotel was highly successful - making so much money that it surely had paid for itself already, the guest rooms were the cleanest in town and the service was GREAT!"* How could so many key front-line team members be so unaware of the real situation? If the key result areas didn't change and turnaround immediately, the hotel might be sold or forced to close - and yet these people didn't realize that their livelihoods were in peril!

Don Smith, professor and former director of Michigan State University's *"The* School of Hospitality Business", has taught me many things. Yet, what I believe to be his most important lesson was this… *"If you are going to win the game, the players must know the score."*

In the case of the hotel in Corpus Christi, we immediately began sharing the monthly financial (P&L) statements, quality assurance reports and copies of all guest correspondence. Every day, the previous day's results were posted and we celebrated increases in occupancy and average daily rates. Quickly, losses were cut in half and soon the hotel regained profitability. By now, the property is indeed probably paid for. I am convinced that by simply letting the players know the score, we were able to win the game.

Southwest Airlines is another excellent company to benchmark with in terms of sharing information. Throughout the turmoil which followed after the tragedy of September 11, 2001 - Southwest Airlines continued to update and saturate its front-line team members with information. Despite the difficulty traveling through airports has become for the general public, and knowing that this low-cost airline actually competes with trains, buses and automobiles on many shorter routes, Southwest is still one of the very few major air carriers that has been able to remain profitable, since.

The management of Southwest Airlines understands that information is power and by letting their team members see an easily understandable scoreboard on a regular basis, they continue to make a difference in the success of the airline as well as to the lives of their customers. Southwest Airlines is known for having happy employees, happy customers and happy investors...all created by *letting the players know the score.*

Chapter 21 - Are You Ready for Business?

"Every morning in Africa, a gazelle wakes up. It knows it must run faster than the fastest lion or it will be killed. Every morning, a lion wakes up. It knows that it must outrun the slowest gazelle or it will starve to death. It doesn't matter whether you are a lion or a gazelle...when the sun comes up, you'd better be running!"
-Neal Hospers, the late Director of the Fort Worth, TX Hotel Association

The hospitality business is one of the most competitive industries there is. Look around, there are dozens and dozens of lodging and food-service choices in virtually every city. Worse, like an airline, hotels and restaurants must realize and deal with that fact that they market/sell a commodity that has a limited shelf-life. For example, if a plane takes off with empty seats the revenue opportunity is lost forever...it is the same thing as if a hotel guest room is left unsold or a restaurant table is left unused and empty at the end of the night.

Jim Potts, former President & CEO of Homestead Studio Suites Hotels understood this competitive nature and he was the key to turning around a struggling company into one of the most successful extended-stay hotel leaders. He would regularly ask team members, *"Are you ready for business?"* This meant that he needed *action,* knowing that action wins games, inaction loses them.

"Ready for business" means that team members make sure to cover the basics, such as a hotel having curb appeal and the rooms spotless. Processes must exist to ensure consistency and continual improvement and the team members are always prepared and committed.

Don Shula, NFL coaching legend used to say, *"More than anything else, over learning - constant practice, constant attention to getting the details right every time - produces a hunger to be in the middle of the action."* In a nutshell, that is the environment being *"ready for business"* creates.

To give a true, real-life example of how being *"ready for business"* translates into increased profitability, let me share the following story from my personal experience. It was June of 1984 and I was the General Manager of a brand new hotel in a suburb of Detroit, Michigan. Though the facility had only been open six weeks, we had trained and practiced over-learning so that all team members could thrive under pressure and be game ready for any moment-of-truth guest interaction.

Upon entering my office one morning, I found a note from Barb Trochim, our Front Desk Guest Service Agent. It said, *"James Buchanan, V.P. of EDS visited the hotel and wants to buy it or at least rent half of it."* Though not excited about the prospect of the new hotel being sold, I did my duty and called the number that was listed on the message.

Mr. Buchanan explained to me that Ross Perot's Electronic Data Systems (EDS) company had just been purchased by General Motors and that they would be relocating tons of people to the Detroit area. He further wanted our hotel to be the headquarters for this move and wished to sign a long-term contract. At the time, I hadn't even heard of Ross Perot (who would later run for President of the United States) nor EDS, but I learned quickly and we negotiated a deal to rent them 50% of the hotel and better yet, they paid-in-full each month…in advance. This resulted in millions of dollars in revenue over the next couple of years.

The most interesting part of the discussion that I had with Mr. Buchanan was when I asked him why he chose our hotel with so many alternatives to choose from, he said, *"I was given the assignment to find our main hotel, along with some others for overflow. I flew in from Dallas and spent the day and night touring various possibilities. Your front desk person, Barb, was the only one who accompanied me down to the rooms I looked at and was the nicest and most well-informed person I met all day. By the time I left, I knew your place was the one we wanted to be at."*

WOW! It has been said that, *"Luck happens when preparation meets opportunity."* That is why, *"Are you ready for business?"* is the most important question to ask yourself & co-workers each day. It could literally be worth millions of dollars to you and whatever organization that you represent.

Chapter 22 - Trim the Fat, Leave the Muscle

*"We cannot do great things on this earth. We can only do
little things with great love."*
-Mother Teresa, 1910-1997, Nobel Peace Prize Recipient

Months before the terrorist attacks of September 11, 2001,
the United States economy was already heading in a
downward spiral. Since then, many businesses, both large
and small, have been experiencing severe financial hardship.
As people fight to survive, everyone is looking for ways to
reduce expenses and do whatever they can to cut costs.
Corporate executives point to newspaper articles announcing
lay-offs, wage freezes and benefit reductions as they search
for ideas to implement within their own organizations.

I have one word of advice. *CAREFUL.* Yes, be careful
when scaling back and trimming off the fat. While these
tough times call for strict fiscal responsibility, they also call
for calm minds and futuristic thinking. Try to envision the
challenges ahead as an opportunity to gain team member and
consumer devotion. Failure to do so can undo years and
years of hard work aimed at building confidence and loyalty.

Remember the movie, *"National Lampoon's Christmas
Vacation,"* starring Chevy Chase as Clark Griswold? While
most people think of the outlandish holiday decorations that
permeate this comedy, it is the underlying theme that is more
sobering. In the film, Griswold's boss falls short of
employee expectations by replacing the annual holiday cash
bonus with a far cheaper, Jelly-of-the-Month Club.
Reminiscent of Ebenezer Scrooge, his boss has a harrowing
experience before learning that while it is okay to trim the
fat, make sure to leave the muscle or else suffer the dire
consequences.

As a hotelier, I am all too aware of the difficult impact that the current economic uncertainty has had on the hospitality industry. Across the country I have heard repeated stories of deepening expense cuts and harsh cost control practices being enacted. As the airlines take away meals on domestic flights and enact additional fees for baggage and ticket changes, some hotels have attempted to reduce amenities, staffing and even linen spending.

While cost control is extremely important to any business, it must also be effective. Trim the fat, but leave the muscle. Here are a couple of examples of what can happen if restraint isn't exercised when implementing expense cuts. First, one popular hotel in Florida actually turned away guests, because the vacant rooms were being left dirty to reduce labor expenditures. When property management was confronted, the answer was, *"My hands are tied, we only get so many minutes to clean per room each week."*

In Georgia, another otherwise excellent hotel facility suffered, not because of a lack of well-trained service personnel, nor a willingness for hard work on the part of the staff. Rather, it all boiled down to a lack of sheets, towels and guest supplies. Team members were sharing vacuum cleaners while waiting for the laundry to be washed and dried and brought back to the storage rooms. Guests requesting additional blankets and pillows were told that none were available by otherwise pleasant front desk team members.

This is not to say that there are not plenty of areas that can easily implement a little belt-tightening. One particular area that can be focused on are the "nice to have" v. "have to have" expenditures. In the hotel business, you have to have people clean the rooms as well as plenty of towels, pillows and blankets to ensure maximum efficiency. On the other hand, you don't need to replace the landscaping pine-straw with mulch. Too many times management will spend funds on items of personal preference, instead of what is truly needed. I have seen many situations where a new manager comes in and wants to replace one type of colorful flower plantings with another. This, at the same time that guests are being told that no extra pillows, irons, hair-dryers, towels, sheets, blankets, shampoo, soap, tissue...you name it, are available. I am not kidding. It happens often.

Speaking of nice to have items that can be scaled back reminds me of a hotel chain that was spending a quarter million dollars annually placing cookies in the lobby, 24 hours a day, at just some locations. Aside from the lack of consistency created when other same-brand locations didn't offer cookies, upper management was shocked to learn that while the guests did enjoy some of them...so did the UPS, FedEx, and U.S. Post Office delivery people, meter readers and other supply vendors. Cookies are good, but only when used to surprise and delight a particular guest experiencing a negative situation or perhaps on a meet-the-management event held periodically. Also, freshly baked cookies can be effective when taken along on sales calls. Yet, cookies that feed those that have no impact on revenues, or are thrown out uneaten, are wasteful.

No matter what company that you are with or business that you are in, there are opportunities to save some money that is currently being spent on frivolity or inefficiencies created by lack of supplies. One thing, though. While trimming the fat, make sure that you aren't also cutting into the muscle. The muscle is what holds your organization together, through both good times and bad, as well. Once all the fat is trimmed, start looking toward increased revenue enhancement opportunities. Sell, sell, sell...that is where to focus next.

Chapter 23 - Everyone Sells!

"Our future success is not the result of two or three key players. Every team member here should feel a sense of accomplishment when a guest walks into our hotel."
-David Lanterman, General Manager, Embassy Suites Hotel-Williamsburg, VA

When I first had the opportunity to work with David Lanterman on a frequent basis, he was the General Manager of a very nice, limited-feature hotel facility located near Cleveland's Hopkins Airport. He caught my attention because he was young, happy, full of energy and oozed enthusiasm. Whatever he did, people enjoyed working with him and were extremely loyal and supportive of his actions.

One reason that David was so popular was that his entire team enjoyed contributing to the success that he enjoyed. He once told me that, *"Everyone is a salesperson, everyone sells."* At his hotel, this was certainly based in fact. On one occasion, his porter, front desk clerk and assistant manager combined together to land a $300,000 account, merely by talking with an in-house guest that was doing some construction work in the area. Soon, this guest's sub-contractors were also staying at the hotel and regularly bringing in 5-10 employees each, for months at a time.

It is extremely important to make outside sales calls in order to increase revenues. Yet, before we go there, let's first make sure that the basics are covered and that we have completely saturated all existing accounts, clients and potential opportunities. As David still says, *"This is where the low-hanging fruit can be found and easily picked for a bountiful harvest."* He is right. If everyone is involved in sales, you will never go hungry.

Let me share two examples of situations that further define the concept of which *everyone sells*. The first situation took place near Chicago, Illinois. I had flown into town to meet with a high-level executive for a fast-food restaurant chain that was doing managerial training with substantial lodging needs for the out-of-town students. He was very satisfied with his current hotel supplier though, in fairness and out of professional courtesy, he agreed to meet with me for an on-site inspection of our nearby hotel facility.

During the course of our conversation, I did everything that I could to sway his decision. I talked about outstanding service, clean rooms, and affordable price. He still wasn't moved enough to make a switch. Desperate, I whisked him away to meet Helen Borski and Judy Reimer in the laundry/storage room of the hotel. This stop was not prearranged, but I knew that it was our last hope to secure his business. Also, I had faith in these two team members.

As we entered the room, Helen immediately rushed over to us and said, *"Hi, Dan! Who is your friend?"* I introduced him and explained that he was a very influential lodging decision-maker for his organization and that we were in process of taking a tour of the hotel and decided to say, *"Hi."* Helen looked him right in the eye and exclaimed, *"That is so exciting! I can tell you one thing, if you bring your people here, you will never regret it. I have been in the hotel business for many years and this is the best hotel in Chicago. Judy and I will take great care of your employees."* I then pointed to the linen shelves containing hundreds of cleaned and folded sheets and towels for the guest rooms. *"This,"* I said, *"is why you should change hotels. Helen and Judy didn't know that you were coming today. You will never find such fine-folded linen at any other hotel. If your people stay here, they will learn about such commitment to excellence."*

We were able to get the large training account, thanks to Helen and Judy. You see, everyone sells. Helen didn't even know that she was selling when she told the client how wonderful we would treat his associates. Judy certainly didn't know that she was selling when she meticulously folded the linens and placed them onto the storage shelves. Still, they closed the deal that I was previously unable to do.

Another example of selling and securing business in your own backyard comes from Eden Prairie, Minnesota. I was meeting with Jo Anne, the General Manager of our hotel there, when a guest stopped me in the lobby and handed me a comment card that said, *"Rita went above and beyond the call of duty, doing some extra things that really helped out...Excellent rating in all categories."* I thanked the guest, turned the card over, and noticed a handwritten note on the backside that said, *"Have a nice day! - Rita."*

So, I asked Jo Anne to take me to see Rita so that I could tell her how much the extra attention and personalized touch meant to this guest, and also to our team. As we spoke, I learned that Rita had been working with us since our facility had opened and that she had previously worked at a nearby, full-service hotel. When Rita switched over to our team, she also provided us with a key sales lead that immediately generated 2,500 room nights for the new facility. WOW!

In all businesses, there are low-hanging fruit opportunities that exist. Make sure that everyone understands that they are highly involved in the sales process, no matter what their specific task might be. Ask existing clients for more business. Ask if they know anyone, like themselves, that might have future potential business. Capitalize on these internal opportunities first, and then put your shoes on. You need to go outside and start pounding the pavement for more!

Chapter 24 - Anatomy of a Successful Sales Call

"Everything you want is out there waiting for you to ask.
Everything you want also wants you. But you have to take
action to get it."
-Jack Canfield, American Motivational Speaker, Author, Trainer

Once an organization consistently produces a high-quality product, regularly exceeds customer service expectations and has completely saturated all existing accounts...it is time to go out and spread the word. In other words, it is time to develop a roadmap or sales plan, and then...*sell like crazy!*

The concept of making outside sales calls was foreign to me when I was going to college. Though there were frequent opportunities to participate in sales blitzes and sales internships, I figured I was going to be a hotel operations guy so there was no reason for me to sign-up. A big mistake.

In 1981, I became General Manager of my first hotel in Lansing, Michigan. The first month had gone well. We quickly received a quality assurance inspection and became ranked #1 in the Central Division in cleanliness and service. That is when the phone rang and my boss told me that I needed to make at least 10 outside sales calls weekly, and set-up a filing system documenting everyone with whom I met.

Yikes! The thought of making outside sales calls gave me sweaty palms. One thing that I did know, if I was going to be good at it, I would need to prepare. Preparation and focus is important in every endeavor and making sales calls is no different. Soon, I learned a very simple 5-Step Sales Process and wrote it down on the back of a business card. Each time that I journeyed out on sales, I would review it. Here it is...

The 5-Step Sales Process

1. Introduction/Establish Rapport.

Once you have fully prepared for making a sales call, by reviewing every detail of information that can be gathered on the prospect, you are now ready to enter the sales meeting.

As a general rule, people are hesitant to meet with a sales person. They are afraid that they will receive a hard-sell sales pitch and then be pressured to make a quick decision. That is why this step is so important. You must penetrate the natural barriers that exist. Quite simply, you just introduce yourself.

Introducing yourself and establishing rapport by briefly discussing a non-business related topic, such as the weather, gives the prospect some time to warm up to you and be more open for the subsequent discussion. I often take a few freshly baked cookies along and introduce myself as a business neighbor just stopping by to say, *"Hi."*

2. Assess Needs.

Of the various sales steps, this is the one that is the most frequently overlooked. Remember, before you can begin selling anything, you must first determine what is important to the potential client. This can be accomplished by asking a series of open-ended questions designed to gain full understanding of their needs, and taking hand-written notes so that you will eventually respond to each area of concern.

In the hotel business, there are many things that can be the key factors influencing a decision to buy. For instance, some people may make their choice strictly on price. Others may be more concerned about location, safety, or whether the facility offers upgraded amenities such as free breakfast, free newspapers and free local telephone calls. Assessing needs allows you to know what is on the mind of your prospect and address each issue of vital importance.

3. Explain Features and Sell Benefits.

Now that you have introduced yourself, established rapport and gained a clear understanding of the needs of your potential client, it is time to explain the features of your product or service and sell the benefits to the prospect.

To assist in this portion of the sales presentation, many people find it is helpful to utilize a professionally produced brochure to help in the process of explaining and describing why it is in the potential client's best interest to buy from you.

Let me give two examples. If service is the most important need of the prospect, discussing letters of endorsement that you have received, comment card or service index ratings would be appropriate. If lowest price is the key determining factor, explaining price in relation to overall value would be what the customer is interested in hearing about.

4. Overcoming Objections.

After you have described the features of your product or service, and have explained to the prospect how it will benefit them to purchase it from you, the next step is to check for understanding and ask additional open-ended questions similar to the assessing needs sales step.

While you might think that you have addressed all areas of

concern, the potential client might not have the same perception. It is very important to check and see if there are any other objections or questions that they might have. Often, this is when the real deal-making begins. For instance, the prospect might say, *"Everything sounds good, except the price is still too high and you need to reduce it another 10% to merit consideration."*

Ouch! Time to go back to more open-ended questions and gain a better understanding of why the price might seem high. *"I am sorry that you feel that the price is too high. Our organization believes in establishing long-term, win-win relationships with our customers. We strive to offer the best value and price relationship. To help me better understand your concern, perhaps you could further explain specifically why the price seems too high?"*

It has been my experience that by being upfront and truly believing in establishing a long-term, win-win relationship, that most obstacles can be overcome. In the above example, offering a lower price might be possible, but only if a specific volume or exclusive relationship is agreed to. Also, it might be that the price doesn't need to be lowered at all, but that the perceived value just needs to be further enhanced.

Regardless, when overcoming obstacles, it is critical to remember that *the important things are seldom urgent and the urgent things are seldom important.* When in doubt, offer to get back with the prospect at a future time and date. This will allow you time to further evaluate the situation.

5. Close the Sale.

Once all of the objections have been overcome and that you and your prospect are ready to reach a deal, it is time to close the sale and ask for the business. Ideally, this initially just involves a quick verbal recap of what has been decided upon, acceptance, and then a finalized written agreement so that everyone completely understands the responsibilities that each party shares.

Sometimes, closing the sale is more difficult. In one case, I remember a prospect who agreed with everything, yet remained hesitant to finalize the deal. In desperation, I asked one final question, *"If you could wave a magic wand and change anything about your current supplier, is there anything that you might change and/or, that we instead, could provide to your organization?"* Instantly, the client mentioned difficulty with trainees cashing expense checks and we were able to work out the final win-win agreement.

So, that is it. This 5-Step Sales Process has always brought me success during any sales meeting. Granted, there are a number of books and training videos that go into far greater detail and have considerable merit. Yet, I prefer to keep things very simple. This really works and get results. You can do it. Write down the steps and place them in your wallet. Commit them to memory and you are on your way to being a successful sales person.

Speaking of being a successful sales person, here are a few additional tips that will make you legendary. First, *make more calls.* If you make 50 calls, you will obtain more business than if you make 25 calls. Next, *go beyond the major accounts.* Most sales people concentrate on the top 10 potential accounts in the marketplace. Go after 11 through 50. Finally, *be persistent.* Get in people's faces and stay there. Sometimes, especially in a difficult economy, it can take as many as five or ten interactions before you get the business. Don't give up. The key to victory might be just around the corner, or on your next sales call. Go get it.

Chapter 25 - Pricing Integrity

*"Progress always involves risk; you can't steal second base
and keep your foot on first."*
-Frederick B. Wilcox, Author

In January of 2003, *Burger King* reluctantly reduced the price of its flagship "Whopper" sandwich to 99 cents. This, in response to declining market share since rival *McDonald's* new Dollar Menu was unveiled, months earlier, featuring the chain's biggest quarter pound burger, "Big N' Tasty," at $1. A friend of mine recently told me that he had enjoyed taking advantage of Burger King's new price reduction over lunch and described it as, *"The Improper Whopper...delicious, with everything on it but the profit."*

The Atlanta Journal Constitution newspaper also followed the burger wars with a headline declaring, *"McDonald's, Burger King wage self-destructive battle."* It reminded me of so many department stores that seemingly felt compelled to cut prices again and again as the 2002 Christmas holiday approached. Lots of sales resulted, yet so did fewer profits.

In the hotel business, many managers seem to rely solely on price reductions to bring in additional guests. Really, if you think about it, I guess the same thing happens in just about any industry. Lowering prices usually does increase short-term revenues. The problem is that this is dangerous and immediately reduces profit margins. Everyone must be reminded that they are in business to make a profit for the organization. Getting back to old-fashion salesmanship, while maintaining pricing integrity, is the direction that I urge everyone to follow.

To give an example of maintaining pricing integrity, let me again refer back to my own experience as a hotelier. In early 1986, I was assigned to be the General Manager of a relatively new hotel in Fenton, Missouri. Fenton is a terrific suburb of St. Louis, and is largely known for having a big automotive plant (conveniently located right across the street from this particular hotel). Yet, unfortunately for our hotel, the people associated with the automotive plant continued to stay miles away at a competitive full-service property.

So, I called up and scheduled an appointment with the lodging coordinator for this large company, then based in Highland Park, Michigan. Surely we could come to some sort of win-win partnership. After all, there was our new, beautiful (but relatively empty) hotel, and the large automaker was at the same time struggling to make a profit. I am not sure, but I think it was the same year that the President of this giant automaker had agreed to work for just $1. Tight expense controls dominated the headlines for this organization. My initial reaction was to cut their room rates to the point that there would be absolutely no competition.

After closely studying the lodging property that had previously secured this business, I decided that our hotel was already the better value. Reducing rates any further would have the decision-makers, and potential guests, question the quality of this new hotel. The problem still existed, though...the rooms were the best value in town, yet remained empty and unused. There had to be a way to convince people to give us a try.

That is when the idea of trial-usage came to mind. Rather than reduce the rate and forever have a negative impact on profits, what about giving them an incredible number of free rooms just to try us out without any sort of obligation. The automaker needed to save money and certainly couldn't refuse such a compelling deal. So, we offered 30 free rooms, each night for the following 45 days. That is right, a potential savings for the automaker of close to $100,000.

Now, this could have worked out to be a lose-win situation for the hotel. Since the rooms were empty anyway, the cost was merely cleaning, utilities and guest supplies. Still, if the guests just used us for the free rooms, and then returned to their former lodging provider, we would have spent a lot of money with nothing to show for it. That is why we decided that these free room recipients would receive strictly VIP treatment. Imagine the look on some of the faces of the automakers executives when the front desk confirmed that their rooms were absolutely free of charge, and then also upgraded them into the very best rooms that were available.

The last few weeks of this trial-usage adventure, the automaker frequently exceeded the 30 free rooms each night. I didn't care. I wanted to become known as the hotel of choice for this automaker and continued to accept whatever reservations that came our way. Funny thing, the day the offer ended, we continued to get all of their business. Except for one thing, now they were paying full rate to stay with us.

There are a couple of lessons to be learned from those days in Fenton, Missouri. The first is that people are creatures of habit and once they feel comfortable with a product or service, they will generally keep utilizing it. The second is that pricing integrity is important in the long-run success of any business. If we had merely cut the room rate deeply, we would have reduced the perceived value of our hotel product and it would have taken years to regain our stature. By giving away the rooms for free, we showed that we were confident in our facility and still maintained pricing integrity.

V. And Then Some...

"These three little words are the secret to success. They are the difference between average people and top people in most companies. The top people always do more than what is expected...and then some. "
-Carl Holmes

"Every time I go out there, I will give 150%...all that I ask of you is 110%. "
-Sammy Davis, Jr., 1925-1990, Entertainer, Member of *"The Rat Pack"*

"Do what you do so well that those who see you do what you do are going to come back and see you do it again and tell others that they should see what you do. "
-Walt Disney, 1901-1966, Co-Founder of the Disney Company

"We must be the change we wish to see in the world. "
-Mahatma Gandhi, 1869-1948, Spiritualist

"It is not what we read, but what we remember that makes us learned. It is not what we intend but what we do that makes us useful. And, it is not a few faint wishes but a lifelong struggle that makes us valiant. "
-Henry Ward Beecher, 1813-1887, Writer

Chapter 26 - Dig Deeper!

"There is something that can happen to every athlete, every human being - it's the instinct to slack off, to give in to pain, to give less than your best...the instinct to hope to win through luck or your opponent's not doing their best, instead of going to the limit, where victory is always found. Defeating those negative instincts that are out to defeat us is the difference between winning and losing, and we face that battle every day of our lives."
-Jesse Owens, 1913-1980, Winner of Four Olympic Gold Medals, 1936

In early 1991, America became increasingly involved in the Persian Gulf War. The prosperity that hoteliers had enjoyed in the 1980's suddenly ceased as tensions heightened and many international firms imposed severe travel restrictions due to the potential of terrorist activities.

One day, during the midst of these troubled times, I was sitting in my relatively comfortable office chair typing another *un*forgettable memo to those who had the pleasure of working with me. Times were tough, but never too tough that another *important* memo couldn't be created...right?

Suddenly, the President of the company appeared standing in front of me and inquired, *"Dan, are we going to make budget in either Chicago or Detroit this week?"* I was shocked by the ridiculous question, surely he was kidding!

"No," I dutifully answered, *"It's been quite some time since we made budget in either of those cities."* He winced, scratched his head, handed me the following passage and asked, *"So, if we aren't going to make budget, why are you here in this office and not in Chicago or perhaps Detroit?"*

DIG DEEPER

Said the little red rooster, "Believe me things are tough.
Seems the worms are scarcer and I cannot find enough.
What's become of all those fat ones is a mystery to me,
There were thousands through that rainy spell, but now
where can they be?"

Then the old black hen who heard him didn't grumble or
complain.
She had gone through lots of dry spells; she had lived
through floods and rain.
So she flew up on the grindstone and she gave her claws a
whet.
As she said, "I've seen the time there weren't worms to get."

She picked a new and undug spot, the earth was hard and
firm.
The little rooster jeered, "New ground - that's no place for a
worm."
The old black hen just spread her feet, she dug both fast and
free,
"I must go to the worms," she said, "the worms won't come
to me."

The rooster vainly spent his day, through habit, by the ways.
Where fat round worms had passed in squads back in the
rainy days.
When nightfall found him supperless, he growled in accents
rough:
"I'm hungry as a fowl can be. Conditions sure are tough."

He turned then to the old black hen and said, "It's worse
with you.
For you're not only hungry, but must be tired too.
I rested while I watched for worms, so I feel fairly perk:
But how are you? Without worms, too - after all that work?"

The old black hen hopped to her perch and dropped her eyes to sleep,
And murmured in a drowsy tone, "Young rooster hear this and weep.
I'm full of worms and happy, for I've eaten like a pig;
The worms are there as always, but boy I had to dig!"

-Author Unknown

I have never forgotten this moment. As I sat alone reading this passage, I realized that the company President was absolutely right. Within minutes I had a plane ticket for Chicago and stopped at home to pack a bunch of clothes...this trip was likely to be a long one.

Whether you are an old black hen, a little red rooster or even a regional hotel manager...the worms are indeed still there. You just have to dig a little harder. It is the same in every industry and every business that I can think of. Never give up and never quit digging. If you ever hear yourself saying, *"But, we are doing everything that we can,"* dig deeper. Trust me, I know...the worms are still there.

Chapter 27 - Relentlessly Making a Difference...

"The itsy bitsy spider went up the water spout,
Down came the rain and washed the spider out.
Out came the sun and dried up all the rain,
And the itsy bitsy spider went up the spout again."
-Children's Nursery Rhyme, Author Unknown

I grew up as the youngest of three Burdakin boys. Mom stayed at home while Dad worked countless hours in the railroad business and eventually became the President of *The Grand Trunk Western Railroad Company* in Detroit, Michigan. The oldest son, John Jr., worked his way through Johns Hopkins University and Wayne State University Medical School becoming a successful and highly regarded Doctor of Medicine in the field of Oncology. The middle son, David, graduated from Lehigh University with a B.S. in Industrial Engineering and then received his MBA degree from Stanford University Graduate School of Business. David is currently President of *The HON Company* and Executive Vice President of *HON Industries*. Look around, if you have a file cabinet or other office equipment, chances are very high that it will have the HON nameplate.

Being the number three son in this household was tough. I remember John, an incredible scholar, being on the high school television show, *"It's Academic."* David also was an outstanding scholar, in addition to being the captain of his high school wrestling and soccer teams. Mom (Radcliffe College graduate) and Dad (Massachusetts Institute of Technology graduate) came from very modest New England backgrounds and strictly enforced rules of traditional etiquette. For instance, wearing a baseball cap (or hat) inside the house was, and still is, generally prohibited.

The point of describing my family's background is that there is one specific trait that this sometimes academically challenged hotel manager did learn while growing up. It is to be *relentless*. No matter what endeavor you might seek, give it your all. Give everything you have. Be relentless. Outwork your peers and your competition. Whether it was my Dad rising up to become a legend in the transportation industry, John becoming a Doctor of Medicine, or David becoming the leader of a large company in Iowa...all were, or still are, relentless. For those who know me and have worked with me in the hotel business, that is why I typically would either be first one in the office in the morning and/or stay and be the last one out in the evening. To *win*, and to *make a difference*, you must be *relentless*.

My family, though now scattered across the United States, still stays in close touch with one another. My brother David once told me about an opportunity that he had to hear Mia Hamm, Gold Medal Winner and U.S. Team Captain of the Olympic Women's Soccer Team, speak about what it takes to be a champion. He noted that the true image of a champion is not the one that automatically comes to mind, the television picture of the winning team doing high fives and hugging after winning the big game.

Rather, Mia Hamm described the true picture of a champion as being in the "shoelace position" after a long day of training. *"Bent over, hands on knees, totally exhausted, soaked with sweat, unable to move, staring at his or her shoelaces."* After a pause, Mia added, *"With absolutely no one else watching."*

So that is what *relentlessly making a difference* is all about. It is going above and beyond, doing the right things and enjoying the inner-rewards of your labor and effort.

Victoria Arbose is a successful Regional Director of Operations for approximately a dozen hotels in the Western United States. She is a friend of mine and someone that cares and goes the extra mile for all of her co-workers and hotel guests. Victoria *relentlessly makes a difference.* The following is an inspirational story that she once passed along to me and I want to share it with you...

MAKING A DIFFERENCE

One day a man was walking along the beach when he noticed a figure in the distance. As he got closer, he realized the figure was that of a boy picking something up and gently throwing it into the ocean. Approaching the boy, he asked "What are you doing?"

The youth replied, "Throwing a starfish into the ocean. The sun is up and the tide is going out. If I don't throw them back, they'll die."

"Son," the man said, "don't you realize there are many miles and miles of beach and hundreds of starfish? You can't possibly make a difference!"

After listening politely, the boy bent down, picked up another starfish and threw it into the surf. Then, smiling at the man, he said, "I made a difference for that one."

(Author Unknown)

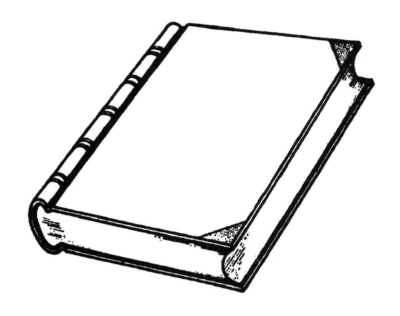

ACKNOWLEDGEMENTS

"You complete me."
-Jerry Maguire (Actor Tom Cruise) in the movie, *"Jerry Maguire"*

Many people have helped me during the creation and writing of *Suite Talk – A Guide to Business Excellence*. It certainly was a team effort and I would also like to thank everyone that provided me the many life experiences that are the foundation of this book.

Art Fettig provided his guidance, wisdom, and book publishing expertise throughout the entire process. I am very grateful for his thoughtful foreword, and I am indebted to Art and his wife, Jean, for their friendship and support.

Many people have taught me so much about the business and world of hospitality management. I would like to thank my professors at Michigan State University, and particularly Ronald Cichy, Michael Kasavana, Raymond Schmidgall and Donald Smith.

I have been fortunate to have had the opportunity to work with, and learn from, many leaders and mentors in the hotel industry. Among these, I would like to express my gratitude to Mark Auerbach, Ken Bednar, Steve Bollinger, Gary DeLapp, Bob Drury, Charles L. Drury, Sr., Chuck Drury, Bruce Edwards, Tom Higgins, Denny Hill, Randy Hulce, Gary Mead, Jim Potts, Chester Reed and John Valletta.

In addition to those named above, I am very appreciative of the many peer relationships that I have enjoyed and learned so much from. These include such wonderful people as Robert Arnold, John Blem, Jim Blomstrom, Rick Blomstrom, Gregg Boyer, Jeff Browning, Brian Brunson,

Mike Carroll, Rhonda Cooling, John Dirnberger, John Dodson, Paul Forman, Tom Fransen, Scott Harvey, Glen Holloway, Bob Kaufman, Sheila King, Debbie Kjellberg, Randy Kluge, Gina Labarre, Amanda Madean, John Malone, Mary McDonald, Greg Morton, Jim Schaefer, Norm Schuessler, Eric Strand, Prudy Stump, Celeste Thompson, David Weiss, Steve Woolridge, Troy Yates and David Ziegler.

Thank you to Gerri Schutes for the cover artwork and her overall assistance in this project.

I would like to thank my Mom and Dad for their constant encouragement and support during the writing of this book and also throughout my entire life.

Most of all, I am beholden to my wife, Cheryl, and my daughter, Nicole. Their combined creativity, intelligence, love, patience and support helped me in countless ways throughout the writing of this book. I could not have done it without them.

About The Author

DAN BURDAKIN has served over twenty years in senior hotel management and is very well known as a leader in the hospitality industry. He has been involved in opening 96 different hotels across the United States, as well as conducting numerous training seminars and meetings.

A 1981 graduate of Michigan State University - *The* School of Hospitality Business, Dan most recently worked as an Executive Vice President for a major all suite, extended-stay hotel chain.

For additional information, bulk purchases and/or other services, you may contact Dan Burdakin directly via the Internet at burdakinhotels@aol.com.

Notes: